NATURAL DECOR

Books by Norma Coney

The Complete Soapmaker

The Complete Candlemaker

Natural Decor

NATURAL DECOR

The Natural Arranger's Garden and Project Book

NORMA CONEY

THE LYONS PRESS

Printed in Spain
10 9 8 7 6 5 4 3 2 1

Design by Catherine Lau Hunt

Library of Congress Cataloging-in-Publication Data

Coney, Norma J., 1955–
Natural decor: the natural arranger's garden and project book / Norma Coney.
p. cm.
Includes index.
ISBN 1-55821-664-2. — ISBN 1-55821-541-7 (pbk.)
1. Floral decorations. 2. Gardening. 3. Nature craft. 4. Flower arrangement in interior decoration. I. Title.
SB449.C6543 1998
745.92—dc21 97-31825
CIP

D.L. TO: 89–1998

CONTENTS

Introduction

The desire to beautify the interior of our homes with nature's bounty is an ancient desire indeed. In our increasingly hurried and modern lifestyle, more and more people feel the need to invite nature inside.

In preceding centuries, however, using natural materials to decorate the interior or exterior of the home took on a much more serious purpose. Plant materials were collected and displayed at very specific times of the year to celebrate the coming of spring, time of harvest, winter solstice, or to convey a message to the viewer. A passerby with a glance at the front door of a cottage could tell if the family was in mourning or feared the influence of evil spirits.

A sheath of wheat was symbolic of riches, fertility, or a bountiful harvest. This symbolism was important because man was totally dependent on natural conditions for his survival. Important plants were treated with reverence. Most of these traditions predate Christianity and in modern times, their origins and intent have been lost. Cultural lines have been smudged, and many plants now have dual meanings, derived from different cultures.

Still, some traditions have survived unscathed through the ages. People still kiss under mistletoe, roses still represent love and affection, and evergreens, symbolic of eternal life, are still used in celebrations that roughly coincide with winter solstice. Many other less obvious traditions persist, perhaps subliminally, as we go about the business of beautifying our homes with natural materials.

Today, the number of natural materials available for use in decorating is astounding.

These materials are sought out and imported from the far corners of the globe. Modern treatments, such as silica drying, freeze drying, and glycerin treatments, have allowed us to utilize many foliages and materials that otherwise would be too fragile or limp to consider. The lure of these exotic plant materials, some of which exhibit extraordinary color patterns or shapes, is hard to resist. Sometimes, however, the price is hard to justify, and one could argue that some treatments leave the materials less than natural looking.

This book will attempt to take you on a journey that I embarked on many years ago, and one that I hope will never end. It is a journey fueled by curiosity, and it takes you on a tour through the natural world in the pursuit of beauty. In this volume we will focus on a wealth of natural materials for you to use in your home. Many of them can be collected in a favorite woodlot, grown in your garden, or purchased from local growers. After you have developed an eye for the materials you will be using, searching them out or growing them becomes half the fun!

You will learn how to grow flowers for drying, as well as how and when to harvest and how to process, dry, and store them. You will also learn how to responsibly collect items from wild places, what to look for, and where to look. Last, you will learn how to present your materials in their best light for use in your arrangements.

I will not inflict on you any strict rules of floral arranging, but will present to you the various techniques and skills that you will need to complete the designs in this book. After completing a few of the suggested designs, working with these materials will come more naturally. Each filler, foliage, or flower has its own feel and personality. As I have told my students for years, mastery of each comes with experience, time, and patience.

The arrangements in this book should serve as inspiration and should spark ideas of your own to try. As you create a piece, it will invariably differ from the one presented in these pages. This is to be expected, and even celebrated, for it is your own personal touch that makes each piece you create truly unique. Go forth . . . and enjoy the trip!

Part 1

Naturals to Grow and Collect

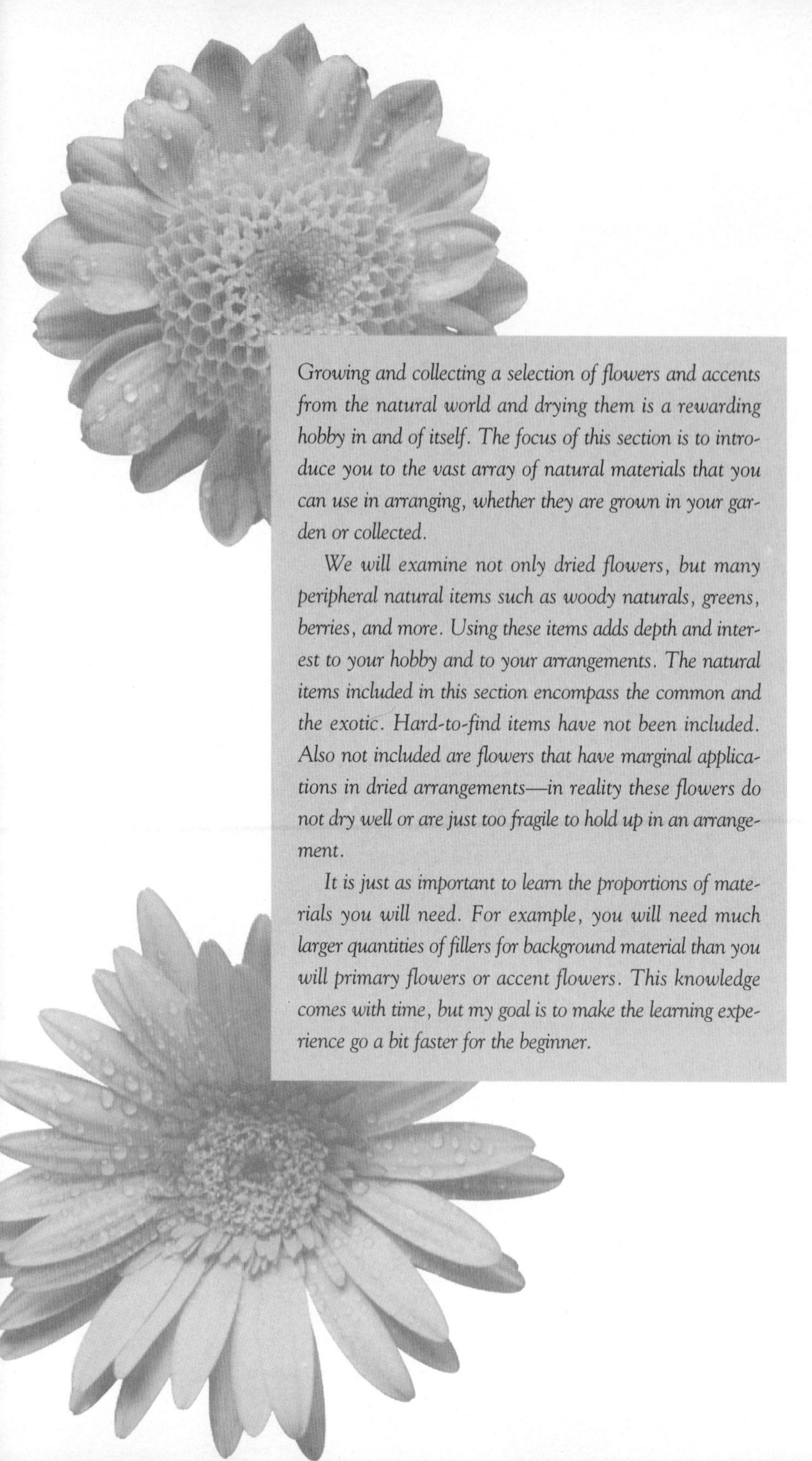

Growing and collecting a selection of flowers and accents from the natural world and drying them is a rewarding hobby in and of itself. The focus of this section is to introduce you to the vast array of natural materials that you can use in arranging, whether they are grown in your garden or collected.

We will examine not only dried flowers, but many peripheral natural items such as woody naturals, greens, berries, and more. Using these items adds depth and interest to your hobby and to your arrangements. The natural items included in this section encompass the common and the exotic. Hard-to-find items have not been included. Also not included are flowers that have marginal applications in dried arrangements—in reality these flowers do not dry well or are just too fragile to hold up in an arrangement.

It is just as important to learn the proportions of materials you will need. For example, you will need much larger quantities of fillers for background material than you will primary flowers or accent flowers. This knowledge comes with time, but my goal is to make the learning experience go a bit faster for the beginner.

A Treasury of Dried Flowers

Dried flowers are the mainstay of any floral arranger's arsenal; they are both natural looking and versatile. Unless you have been arranging for some time, you may not realize how dried flowers fit into the arrangements that you will be making. Generally, dried flowers fall into one of three categories: **fillers, primary flowers,** or **secondary flowers.**

In the natural world, flowers that can be used as fillers, or background material, are few and far between. Fillers are used to create the base of the arrangement that you are making—and therefore they influence the style and feel of the piece. In a wreath, for example, the filler will provide the base for you to build on; it must be sturdy and create an attractive backdrop for the primary flowers that are featured in the wreath. This does not necessarily mean that fillers are devoid of character. On the contrary, each one has a personality that is twofold: Each has its own beautiful and unique look, and each reacts differently when you work with it.

Primary flowers are the flowers that will be showcased in your arrangement. They jump out at you visually and are larger than secondary flowers—sometimes so large that they cannot be ignored. Perhaps they have a striking form, shape, or color that makes them stand out. Whatever the case, these flowers will provide the focus of your piece, and any other flowers you use will have to complement them in form and color.

Secondary flowers are the flowers that we use to accent or complement the primary flowers in a given arrangement. They may be neutral or bold in color, but are usually smaller and more delicate than the primary flowers. In most cases, they provide just the right touch to finish an arrangement by bringing out a color or texture that otherwise would be less noticeable.

Having said all this, I must warn you: Dried flowers and other natural materials do not always fall into these neat categories. The idea here is to gain the experience that will help you figure the general proportions in which you will need to grow these flowers to execute the designs you choose to make, *not to become overly concerned about where the flowers fit into these categories*.

FILLERS

In this listing, USDA zonal information has been given only for perennial plants.

COMMON NAME: Baby's breath.
LATIN NAME: *Gypsophila paniculata.*
CLASSIFICATION: Perennial to zone 3.
COLOR: White.
CONDITIONS: Full sun in well-drained soil.
BEST METHOD: Buy mature plants.
EASE OF GROWTH: Easy in well-drained soil.
HARVEST TIME AND METHOD: July. Harvest when individual flowers open; bundle and hang to air dry.
PREPARATION: Use natural or spray with floral paint.

Baby's breath.

COMMENTS: Seedlings can take up to four years to produce flowers; each plant needs a four foot by four foot area in which to grow; this plant resents being moved.

COMMON NAME: German statice.
LATIN NAME: *Goniolimon tataricum.*

German statice.

CLASSIFICATION: Perennial to zone 4.
COLOR: White with lavender blue centers.
CONDITIONS: Full sun in very well-drained soil.
BEST METHOD: Buy well-established seedlings or nearly mature plants.
EASE OF GROWTH: Can be difficult and unpredictable, even in loamy well-drained soils.
HARVEST TIME AND METHOD: July. Pick as soon as individual flowers open on the stalks. Bundle and hang to air dry.
PREPARATION: Use natural; if statice should brown out, it can be dyed with fabric or floral dye.
COMMENTS: This is a very difficult plant to grow; if you have poorly drained soil it will be nearly impossible to produce a crop; reacts by browning if dry weather is prevalent near harvest; plants die off unpredictably even in the best conditions; resents competition from weeds.

COMMON NAME: Sea lavender, statice latifolia.
LATIN NAME: *Limonium latifolium.*
CLASSIFICATION: Perennial to zone 3.
COLOR: White with lavender centers.
CONDITIONS: Any good garden soil, well drained.
BEST METHOD: Purchase plants.
EASE OF GROWTH: Easy except in heavy soil.
HARVEST TIME AND METHOD: July. Harvest as soon as individual flowers start to open. Bundle and hang to air dry.
PREPARATION: Use natural or spray lightly with a floral spray.

Lavender.

COMMON NAME: Silver King artemisia.
LATIN NAME: *Artemisia.*
CLASSIFICATION: Perennial to zone 3.
COLOR: Silvery gray.
CONDITIONS: Average garden soil.
BEST METHOD: Purchase plants to be sure that you are buying the variety "Silver King"—the best for drying.
EASE OF GROWTH: Easy in nearly any soil.
HARVEST TIME AND METHOD: August or September. Cut the upper 36 inches of stalk; bundle in small bunches to air dry, or loosely stand the stalks up in large boxes.

PREPARATION: Natural.

COMMENTS: The tips of the stalks are the most sought after part of this plant (the flowers contained there are inconspicuous); this plant can be very invasive and is best planted by itself rather than in a garden setting.

COMMON NAME: Sweet Annie.

LATIN NAME: *Artemisia annua.*

CLASSIFICATION: Annual.

COLOR: Olive green to gold.

CONDITIONS: Average garden soil.

BEST METHOD: Buy seedlings or start plants from seed.

EASE OF GROWTH: Easy.

HARVEST TIME AND METHOD: August or September. Cut the entire plant at the base and hang upside down.

PREPARATION: Natural.

COMMENTS: Sweet Annie gets its name from the incredibly sweet fragrance produced by lightly brushing it with your fingertips. While most people adore this fragrance, it is possible to become allergic to it. This usually happens only after years of working with it for long periods of time in areas where the ventilation is not the best. Sweet Annie poses little threat to anyone who works with it sporadically, and once an arrangement is hung, the fragrance is not released as easily, yet it can lightly perfume a room.

Sweet Annie, baby's breath, and Silver King.

The saying goes that once you have Sweet Annie in your garden, you will never be without it again! It self-sows readily and without your prior consent.

PRIMARY FLOWERS

COMMON NAME: Anise hyssop.
LATIN NAME: *Agastache Foeniculum.*
CLASSIFICATION: Perennial zone 5 or 6.
COLOR: Lavender blue.
CONDITIONS: Average garden soil.
BEST METHOD: Purchase plants or grow from seed.
EASE OF GROWTH: Easy.
HARVEST TIME AND METHOD: June through September. Cut on the stem and bundle loosely to air dry by hanging. If you do not want the stem, cut individual flowers and dry on a screen.
PREPARATION: Natural.
COMMENTS: Anise hyssop may travel around the garden (in cold climates plants can sometimes die out seemingly without reason); the solution to this problem is to let one plant set seed in the garden each season. These seedlings will bloom the first year and you will not miss a harvest or have to replace plants.

COMMON NAME: Annual statice.
LATIN NAME: *Limonium sinuatum.*
CLASSIFICATION: Annual.
COLOR: White, yellow, lavender, pale pink, rose, carmine, violet, and salmon.
CONDITIONS: Good garden soil.
BEST METHOD: Grow your own transplants to assure that you get the colors you desire.
EASE OF GROWTH: Easy.
HARVEST TIME AND METHOD: Plants begin to yield in late June or July. Harvest as soon as the individual flowers are open. Harvest only the stalks on which flowers are open; partially open statice flowers will not open as they dry. Bundle loosely and hang upside down to air dry.
PREPARATION: Natural.

COMMON NAME: Cockscomb.
LATIN NAME: *Celosia argentea*, var. *cristata* and *plumosa*.
CLASSIFICATION: Annual.
COLOR: Red, magenta, gold, or pink.
CONDITIONS: Good garden soil.
BEST METHOD: Grow your own transplants or buy plants.
EASE OF GROWTH: Moderately difficult.
HARVEST TIME AND METHOD: July through August. Harvest flowers when full color has developed. Cut the stem and hang singly to air dry.
PREPARATION: Natural.
COMMENTS: There are two types of cockscomb: Crested cockscomb has a tightly curled flower head; plume cockscomb has a loose plume-like flower. Although cockscomb is beautiful and commands attention, the color tends to fade very quickly. Best results may be had by dying the heads with fabric dye.

COMMON NAME: Globe amaranth.
LATIN NAME: *Gomphrena globosa*, *Gomphrena Haageana*.
CLASSIFICATION: Annual.
COLOR: Pink, rose, white, fuchsia, red, or orange.
CONDITIONS: Good garden soil.
BEST METHOD: Grow your own transplants.
EASE OF GROWTH: Easy once plants are established.
HARVEST TIME AND METHOD: July. This plant thrives on heat and for those of us in northern climates, this can occasionally be a problem—it will not produce many flowers until the weather is right. There are two methods of harvesting globe amaranth. The first is to let the flowers grow to their ultimate size—which is quite large—and then cut the stalk and hang it. This method will net you a few large flowers, and some smaller ones. It will take the plant a long time to produce again—in northern climates, the plants may not have time to develop more flowers. The second method of harvest is to pluck the flowers from the plant in the same way that strawflower is harvested. This will bring you a multitude of smaller, high-quality flowers that will be cut and come again until a frost ends the season. If you allow the flowers to develop, they will not become what is called fully blown like many other dried flowers, they will just be larger when you do get around to picking them. (Sometimes fully blown centers will look clean, but most times they will look soiled and are inferior.) Flowers harvested using the second method may be dried on a screen.

COMMENTS: This flower is favored above all others by mice as a nest, so once your flowers have dried, store them securely in a plastic container or plastic bag.

PREPARATION: Natural.

COMMON NAME: Globe thistle.

LATIN NAME: *Echinops Ritro, E. sphaerocephalus.*

CLASSIFICATION: Perennial to zone 3.

COLOR: Steel blue.

CONDITIONS: Average garden soil.

BEST METHOD: Purchase plants or grow from seed.

EASE OF GROWTH: Easy.

HARVEST TIME AND METHOD: June through July. Cut the flower heads as soon as they show blue color. Bundle in loose bunches and hang upside down to air dry.

PREPARATION: Natural.

COMMENTS: The shape of these thistle-like flowers is unusual and interesting. Globe thistle is not terribly durable; handle flower heads with care.

COMMON NAME: Hydrangea.

LATIN NAME: *Hydrangea paniculata.*

Pearly everlasting and hydrangea.

CLASSIFICATION: Shrub to zone 3.
COLOR: Beige or white blushed with mauve.
CONDITIONS: Average garden soil.
BEST METHOD: Purchase an established shrub.
EASE OF GROWTH: Easy.
HARVEST TIME AND METHOD: August through October. Cut short stems from the shrub and air dry on a screen. Bunches can be hung, but they take up a lot of air space.
PREPARATION: Natural; flower heads that have lost their color can sometimes be revived by dyeing them with a floral dip and rinse-type dye. Sometimes good results can be had with fabric dye; floral spray paints look unnatural.
COMMENTS: This is the most reliable hydrangea for drying. In warm climates, blue hydrangeas may be available. Hydrangea must be picked after the flowers have **hardened.** This means that some moisture has left the flowers and they are no longer **soft.** If harvested too early, they will wilt. The mauve blush is obtained late in the season as cold night temperatures bring this color forward. If frost hits early before cold temperatures have had a chance to bring out the color, the flowers for that season will be green and beige.

COMMON NAME: Pearly everlasting.
LATIN NAME: *Anaphalis margaritacea*, *A. yedoensis*.
CLASSIFICATION: Perennial to zone 3.
COLOR: White.
CONDITIONS: Average garden soil.
BEST METHOD: Purchase plants.
EASE OF GROWTH: Easy.
HARVEST TIME AND METHOD: July through August. Cut stems about one foot long, bundle, and air dry; or pluck flower heads from the stem and dry on a screen.
PREPARATION: Natural; flowers not in peak condition can be dyed with fabric dye.
COMMENTS: Flowers need to be kept tightly bunched to look good in any arrangement. Gather a small number of stems, and with your fingers, pinch the flowers together and roll them until you get a nice full bunch.

COMMON NAME: Rose.

LATIN NAME: *Rosa* species.

CLASSIFICATION: Shrub.

COLOR: Red, pink, salmon, white, lavender, fuchsia, or yellow.

CONDITIONS: Good garden soil.

BEST METHOD: Purchase plants.

EASE OF GROWTH: Can be difficult in some climates.

HARVEST TIME AND METHOD: Pluck buds or tight blooms at peak. If on a stem, bundle loosely and air dry. Individual flowers may be dried on a screen.

PREPARATION: Natural.

COMMENTS: Roses bloom sporadically after their main bloom time, so you can harvest as the season goes along. Some varieties are easier to grow than others; in some climates you may have to settle for small flowers. For recommendations of what roses to grow in your area, consult an experienced gardener whose judgment you can trust.

COMMON NAME: Sea holly.

LATIN NAME: *Eryngium*, various species.

CLASSIFICATION: Perennials, most to zone 5.

COLOR: Steel blue, silvery blue, or gray.

CONDITIONS: Well-drained garden soil.

BEST METHOD: Purchase established plants.

EASE OF GROWTH: Easy once established.

HARVEST TIME AND METHOD: June through July. Cut individual stems and hang to air dry.

PREPARATION: Natural; faded flower heads may be sprayed lightly with floral paint.

COMMON NAME: Strawflower.

LATIN NAME: *Helichrysum bracteatum* (Monstrosum Bikini).

CLASSIFICATION: Annual.

COLOR: White, rose, pink, mauve, burgundy, sulphur yellow, orange, red, brown, russet, or gold.

CONDITIONS: Good garden soil.

BEST METHOD: Grow your own transplants to get the colors you most desire.

EASE OF GROWTH: Easy once germinated.

HARVEST TIME AND METHOD: To harvest, *don't* cut the stem as is widely advised! This cuts off many future flowers, and the stem tissue you cut takes weeks to grow back. Pluck the flowers off the top of the stem. Harvest flowers before they open fully or they will have fully blown centers and they will not be as attractive as flowers that have been harvested properly. If you use this method your planting will be "cut and come again," meaning that you can go back to the planting in about one week's time and find a new crop to harvest. Spread flowers on a screen in your drying area in a single layer.

PREPARATION: Natural.

COMMON NAME: Sunflower.

LATIN NAME: *Helianthus annuus.*

CLASSIFICATION: Annual.

COLOR: Shades of yellow, gold, orange, or red.

CONDITIONS: Average garden soil.

BEST METHOD: Sow seed.

EASE OF GROWTH: Easy.

HARVEST TIME AND METHOD: July through September. Cut flower heads at their peak—they can be hung individually or dried flat on a screen. Hanging produces a less perfect flower, but one with charm.

PREPARATION: Natural.

COMMON NAME: Tansy.

LATIN NAME: *Tanacetum vulgare.*

CLASSIFICATION: Perennial to zone 4.

COLOR: Golden yellow.

CONDITIONS: Average garden soil.

BEST METHOD: Purchase plants.

EASE OF GROWTH: Easy.

HARVEST TIME AND METHOD: July. Cut the stem, hang in loose bunches, and air dry.

PREPARATION: Natural; buttons may be dyed with fabric dye.

COMMENTS: This plant can be somewhat invasive; plant by itself away from the garden.

COMMON NAME: Yarrow.
LATIN NAME: *Achillea filipendulina*.
CLASSIFICATION: Perennial to zone 3.
COLOR: Yellow or gold.
CONDITIONS: Average garden soil.
BEST METHOD: Purchase plants.
EASE OF GROWTH: Easy.
HARVEST TIME AND METHOD: June. Harvest as soon as flower heads show that they have developed full color. Bundle and hang to air dry.
PREPARATION: Natural.

Yarrow.

ACCENT FLOWERS

COMMON NAME: Achillea the pearl.
LATIN NAME: *Achillea ptarmica*.
CLASSIFICATION: Perennial to zone 4.
COLOR: White.
CONDITIONS: Average garden soil.
BEST METHOD: Purchase plants.
EASE OF GROWTH: Easy.

HARVEST TIME AND METHOD: Throughout the growing season. Harvest when flowers are fresh and white for best color when dry. Cut stems and bundle loosely; hang upside down to air dry.
PREPARATION: Natural.
COMMENTS: This plant is a good substitute for annual baby's breath (which is not included in this book because it is so difficult to grow). The flower heads retain their size when dry. This plant wanders a bit in the garden, so you may want to give it a corner to expand in away from more delicate plants.

COMMON NAME: Astilbe.
LATIN NAME: *Astilbe*, various cultivars.
CLASSIFICATION: Perennial to zone 4.
COLOR: Red, pink, lavender, or white.
CONDITIONS: Rich garden soil.
BEST METHOD: Purchase plants.
EASE OF GROWTH: Easy once established.
HARVEST TIME AND METHOD: June through August, depending on variety. Cut plumes and hang upside down in small bunches to air dry.
PREPARATION: Natural.

COMMON NAME: Bee balm, Oswego tea.
LATIN NAME: *Monarda didyma*.
CLASSIFICATION: Perennial to zone 4.
COLOR: Red, pink, rose, white, or violet.
CONDITIONS: Average garden soil with ample moisture.
BEST METHOD: Purchase plants to be sure that you get the color you desire.
EASE OF GROWTH: Easy.
HARVEST TIME AND METHOD: July through August. Harvest flowers as soon as they open; bundle in small bunches and hang upside down to air dry.
PREPARATION: Natural.

COMMON NAME: Chives.
LATIN NAME: *Allium Schoenoprasum*.
CLASSIFICATION: Perennial to zone 3.
COLOR: Lavender pink.
CONDITIONS: Average garden soil.
BEST METHOD: Seed or purchase plants.
EASE OF GROWTH: Easy.
HARVEST TIME AND METHOD: May. Cut flower stems just as they begin to open. Bundle in small bunches and hang upside down to air dry.
PREPARATION: Natural.

COMMON NAME: Field yarrow.
LATIN NAME: *Achillea millefolium*.
CLASSIFICATION: Perennial to zone 3.
COLOR: White.
CONDITIONS: Average garden soil.
BEST METHOD: Purchase or collect plants.
EASE OF GROWTH: Easy.
HARVEST TIME AND METHOD: June. Pick flowers as they open. Bundle to hang upside down for air drying, or place individual flowers facedown on a screen to dry.
PREPARATION: Natural or flowers can be dyed with fabric or floral dye.
COMMENTS: Yarrow, although somewhat fragile, is a nice flower to use between primary flowers because of its ivory color. Another species, *Achillea taygetea*, has colored flower heads. Although they are pretty in the garden, they do not hold their color very well when dried. Field yarrow is best put in a location where it can be by itself, as it tends to be a bit invasive.

COMMON NAME: Immortelle.
LATIN NAME: *Xeranthemum annuum*.
CLASSIFICATION: Annual.
COLOR: Pale pink lavender and white.
CONDITIONS: Average garden soil.
BEST METHOD: Start your own transplants from seed.

EASE OF GROWTH: Easy.

HARVEST TIME AND METHOD: July through September. Cut stems and bundle loosely; hang upside down to air dry.

PREPARATION: Natural.

COMMON NAME: Larkspur, delphinium.

LATIN NAME: *Consolida* species, *Delphinium* species.

CLASSIFICATION: Annual, biennial, or perennial.

COLOR: White, pink, or blue.

CONDITIONS: Good garden soil.

BEST METHOD: Purchase established plants.

EASE OF GROWTH: Difficult.

HARVEST TIME AND METHOD: July through October. Cut entire stem just before flowers are fully open. Hang individually to air dry.

PREPARATION: Natural.

COMMENTS: Delphiniums and larkspur are difficult plants. Slugs damage even the mature plants. Plants are short-lived and seem to die out for no apparent reason.

COMMON NAME: Lavender.

LATIN NAME: *Lavandula angustifolia* and other species.

CLASSIFICATION: Perennial to zone 5.

COLOR: Violet, blue, or white/pink.

CONDITIONS: Well-drained soil.

BEST METHOD: Purchase plants that will be winter-hardy in your area.

EASE OF GROWTH: Easy once established.

HARVEST TIME AND METHOD: June through July. Cut flower stalks as soon as they open. Bundle and hang upside down to air dry.

PREPARATION: Natural.

COMMENTS: Lavender is not difficult to grow if you have well-drained soil. It loves a yearly application of lime. If you have trouble getting plants to survive the winter they are either too wet or the wrong variety for your area.

COMMON NAME: Lavender cotton.
LATIN NAME: *Santolina Chamaecyparissus*.
CLASSIFICATION: Perennial to zone 5.
COLOR: Yellow.
CONDITIONS: Well-drained soil.
BEST METHOD: Purchase plants.
EASE OF GROWTH: Easy, except in extreme northern climates with cold, windy winters.
HARVEST TIME AND METHOD: June. Cut flower stalks, bundle, and hang upside down to air dry.
PREPARATION: Natural. They also take dye very well.

COMMON NAME: Queen of the meadow.
LATIN NAME: *Filipendula Ulmaria*.
CLASSIFICATION: Perennial to zone 4.
COLOR: Ivory.
CONDITIONS: Good garden soil.
BEST METHOD: Purchase plants.
EASE OF GROWTH: Easy.
HARVEST TIME AND METHOD: July. Cut plumes and hang upside down in small bunches.
PREPARATION: Natural.

COMMON NAME: Salvia.
LATIN NAME: *Salvia farinacea*.
CLASSIFICATION: Annual.
COLOR: Violet or white.
CONDITIONS: Average garden soil.
BEST METHOD: Purchase plants.
EASE OF GROWTH: Easy.
HARVEST TIME AND METHOD: Harvest throughout the summer. Cut flower stems when flowers open. Bundle and hang upside down to air dry.
PREPARATION: Natural.

COMMON NAME: White mugwort.
LATIN NAME: *Artemisia lactiflora.*
CLASSIFICATION: Perennial to zone 4.
COLOR: White.
CONDITIONS: Average garden soil.
BEST METHOD: Purchase plants.
EASE OF GROWTH: Easy.
HARVEST TIME AND METHOD: July through August. Cut stalks and hang upside down to air dry.
PREPARATION: Natural.

COMMON NAME: Wild quinine.
LATIN NAME: *Parthenium integrifolium.*
CLASSIFICATION: Perennial to zone 4 or 5.
COLOR: Ivory.
CONDITIONS: Good garden soil.
BEST METHOD: Purchase established plants.
EASE OF GROWTH: Easy once established.
HARVEST TIME AND METHOD: July through August. Cut stems and hang in loose bunches upside down to air dry.

Larkspur, salvia, chives, monarda, wild quinine, lavender, and agastache.

PREPARATION: Natural or can be dyed.

COMMENTS: This lovely prairie plant is a wonderful complement to other dried flowers.

COMMON NAME: Winged everlasting.

LATIN NAME: *Ammobium alatum*.

CLASSIFICATION: Annual.

COLOR: White with yellow centers.

CONDITIONS: Average garden soil.

BEST METHOD: Start your own transplants.

EASE OF GROWTH: Easy.

HARVEST TIME AND METHOD: July through September. Pluck or cut fresh individual flowers from the stems, or cut and bundle the stems, hanging them upside down to air dry. If you pluck individual flowers, spread them on a screen to dry.

PREPARATION: Natural.

COMMENTS: This flower can be difficult to harvest because the stems sprawl and twist, and bending over to pick the flowers is strenuous—especially if you have a lot of plants. A new variety called "bikini" is supposed to be a dwarf, making the job more pleasant.

2 Foliages, Grasses, and Herbs

Foliage is very important to the floral arranger. It adds interest, contrast, depth, and natural beauty to any floral piece. Although all foliage is beautiful, durability is a different matter: There are not many types of foliage that can hold up to the amount of handling necessary to make an arrangement.

Another quirk about foliage is that it is not thought of as something arrangers would grow themselves, as so many foliages require special treatments in order to be used. Yet, there are a few that can be grown easily in the landscape or acquired by other means.

If a given plant cannot be grown at home, I have substituted a method of acquiring the plant for the purpose of this listing. Color and growing conditions have been indicated only where applicable.

FOLIAGES

The key to choosing foliage for an arrangement is not only using what will look good, but using what will be durable in a given arrangement. Keep in mind that foliage will take less abuse in a wreath that hangs than it will in a centerpiece that sits on a tabletop.

COMMON NAME: Asparagus fern.
LATIN NAME: *Asparagus densiflorus* "Sprengeri."
CLASSIFICATION: Perennial—grown as a houseplant.
COLOR: Bright medium green.
BEST METHOD: Purchase treated fern from a floral supply center.
COMMENTS: Asparagus fern is difficult to grow and treat at home, but it is a nice delicate foliage and is more durable than its appearance would have you believe.

COMMON NAME: Bracken fern.
LATIN NAME: *Pteridium* species.
CLASSIFICATION: Perennial to zone 3.
COLOR: Medium green.
CONDITIONS: Usually found growing in fields and woods.
BEST METHOD: Collect stems of bracken from the wild.
HARVEST TIME AND METHOD: Harvest any time after the stalks have fully developed in the spring. Treat immediately, or dry by hanging bunches upside down.
PREPARATION: Bracken fern can be treated so that it can, in a pinch, serve as a wreath base. The fern stems should be dyed with fabric dye—a small amount of glycerin should be added to the dye bath to keep the foliage from becoming brittle.

COMMON NAME: Boxwood.
LATIN NAME: *Buxus* species.

Boxwood, running cedar, asparagus fern, and princess pine.

Classification: Shrub zone 5.
Color: Medium green.
Conditions: Average garden soil and full sun. Boxwood does not like dry, cold, winter winds.
Best method: Grow your own or buy a case from a floral supplier.
Ease of growth: Easiest in humid, mild climates.
Harvest time and method: Cut lengths of foliage early enough so that the wood can heal before winter.
Preparation: Boxwood can be used in fresh arrangements or dried by spreading it on a screen. Boxwood can be dyed hunter green with fabric dye when it is fresh or dry.

Common name: Cedar.
Latin name: *Cedrus* species and *Juniperus* species.
Classification: Tree or shrub.
Color: Various shades of green and blue-green.
Conditions: Cedar are commonly found in landscapes and parks.
Best method: Cut small branches from shrubs in your landscape or where you have gained permission to collect.
Preparation: Use in the natural state or treat with fabric dye and a small amount of glycerin.

Common name: Dusty miller.
Latin name: *Cineraria maritima* or *Pyrethrum* species.
Classification: Annual.
Color: Silver.
Conditions: Average garden soil and full sun.
Best method: Purchase transplants.
Ease of growth: Easy.
Harvest time and method: July through October. Cut stalks, bundle loosely, and hang upside down to air dry.
Preparation: Natural.
Comments: If you like dusty miller but do not want to bother with planting annuals every year, see Artemisia (page 26).

COMMON NAME: English ivy.

LATIN NAME: *Hedera Helix*.

CLASSIFICATION: Perennial zone 5.

COLOR: Deep green, light green, golden green, or numerous combinations of variegation.

CONDITIONS: Average garden soil. It can also be grown indoors in pots.

BEST METHOD: Purchase plants with leaf color and texture that please you.

EASE OF GROWTH: Easy.

HARVEST TIME AND METHOD: Harvest whenever the vine is long enough to cut a substantial amount of foliage off. Dry lengths of vine flat on a screen.

PREPARATION: Once dry, ivy can be spray-painted with a light coat of metallic gilding to add an elegant touch to any wreath. Lengths of vine may be dyed hunter green with fabric dye when still green.

COMMENTS: While ivy will not be the mainstay that some other foliages are, it can add a nice touch to any arrangement.

COMMON NAME: Eucalyptus.

LATIN NAME: *Eucalyptus cinerea* and other species.

CLASSIFICATION: Tree, grown as an annual in the north.

COLOR: Deep green, blue green, reddish brown, or silver-green.

CONDITIONS: Average garden soil.

BEST METHOD: Purchase pretreated bunches of foliage.

COMMENTS: Eucalyptus can sometimes be grown in the garden, but you will not be able to treat it successfully with glycerin at home. Untreated foliage can be used in arrangements, but will be somewhat more brittle and will retain its natural color. When buying eucalyptus, look for lots of branching and branches that do not have huge stems—these will be more difficult to use in arrangements. Also beware of browning on the edges of the leaves.

COMMON NAME: Heather.

LATIN NAME: *Calluna vulgaris*.

CLASSIFICATION: Perennial shrub.

COLOR: Pink.

BEST METHOD: Purchase lush, fresh, flowering stems from a floral supply center.

PREPARATION: Natural.

COMMENTS: Heather can be a bit brittle when dry, so handle it with care and do not use it in arrangements that are likely to be jostled once they are placed.

COMMON NAME: Leather leaf fern.
LATIN NAME: *Rumohra adiantiformis*.
CLASSIFICATION: Perennial.
COLOR: Deep green.
BEST METHOD: Purchase foliage bunches from a floral supply center.
PREPARATION: Leather leaf can be treated reasonably well with glycerin and fabric dye.
COMMENTS: Leather leaf makes a wonderful foliage background for flowers.

COMMON NAME: Lemon leaf, salal.
LATIN NAME: *Gaultheria Shallon*.
CLASSIFICATION: Shrub.
COLOR: Olive green.
CONDITIONS: Grows wild from the Alaskan coast into coastal California to zone 6.
BEST METHOD: Collect only where you have permission. Purchase bunches from a floral supply center.
PREPARATION: Natural, or individual leaves can be dyed with fabric dye.

COMMON NAME: Magnolia.
LATIN NAME: *Magnolia grandiflora* and other species.
CLASSIFICATION: Tree.
COLOR: Deep glossy green.
CONDITIONS: Magnolias are common trees in the southern United States.
BEST METHOD: Cut short branches from trees any time after the foliage has hardened.
PREPARATION: Use natural, or dye with fabric dye.

COMMON NAME: Princess pine.

LATIN NAME: *Crassula* or *Lycopodium* species.

CLASSIFICATION: Perennial to zone 4.

COLOR: Christmas green.

CONDITIONS: Usually found growing in acid soils in wooded or nearly wooded areas.

BEST METHOD: Purchase lengths of garland at Christmas or purchase leftover stock just after the holidays. Collect only when permission has been given to collect from private land.

PREPARATION: Princess pine garland can be dyed hunter green with fabric dye and can be made into wreaths while it is still pliable.

COMMON NAME: Running cedar.

LATIN NAME: *Lycopodium digitatum*.

CLASSIFICATION: Perennial to zone 4.

COLOR: Bright green.

CONDITIONS: Usually found growing in acidic soils in wooded or nearly wooded areas.

BEST METHOD: Collect selectively from private land only when permission has been granted.

PREPARATION: Running cedar can be dyed with fabric dye and a small amount of glycerin, then made into wreaths or garlands while it is still pliable.

HERB FOLIAGES

COMMON NAME: Artemisia, Old woman.

LATIN NAME: *Artemisia Stellerana*.

CLASSIFICATION: Perennial to zone 5.

COLOR: Silver.

CONDITIONS: Well-drained garden soil.

BEST METHOD: Purchase plants.

EASE OF GROWTH: Easy.

HARVEST TIME AND METHOD: June through October. Cut stems and use fresh, or bundle and hang upside down to air dry.

PREPARATION: Natural, fresh or dried.

COMMENTS: This foliage looks like dusty miller (page 23).

COMMON NAME: Lamb's ears.
LATIN NAME: *Stachys byzantina.*
CLASSIFICATION: Perennial to zone 5.
COLOR: Silver.
CONDITIONS: Any garden soil.
BEST METHOD: Purchase plants.
EASE OF GROWTH: Easy.
HARVEST TIME AND METHOD: July. Cut stalks while the flowers are still fresh, bundle, and hang upside down to air dry. Leaves may be harvested any time of year; dry in small bunches or flat on a screen.
PREPARATION: Natural.

Lamb's ear, sage, artemisia stelleaner, and ivy.

COMMON NAME: Sage.
LATIN NAME: *Salvia officinalis.*
CLASSIFICATION: Perennial to zone 5.
COLOR: Gray-green.
CONDITIONS: Well-drained garden soil.
BEST METHOD: Purchase young plants.
EASE OF GROWTH: Easy.
HARVEST TIME AND METHOD: June through September. Cut stems, bundle, and hang upside down to air dry; or lay stems neatly on a screen to dry.
PREPARATION: Natural.

COMMENTS: Sage can be used fresh if you need to bend the stems—to make a wreath, for example. It can also be used well after it is dried.

GRASSES

Many grasses have ornamental seed heads that are useful in arrangements. Some of these grasses grow wild or on the side of the road and can be collected easily. Others that are not native to your area can be acquired for your garden.

A word of caution: Beware of grasses, wild or otherwise, that have invasive habits. Invasive grasses usually spread one of two ways: through an invasive root system or through dispersing unbelievable amounts of seed. If you see a grass you like but notice that it has taken over the area in which it is growing, that is a good sign that the grass will not behave well in your garden. You may wish instead to plant it somewhere that is totally separate from your garden, or you may wish to continue to collect it from the wild.

Grasses to Grow

COMMON NAME: Bearded wheat.
LATIN NAME: *Triticum* species.
CLASSIFICATION: Annual.
COLOR: Pale straw yellow.
CONDITIONS: Good garden soil.
BEST METHOD: Sow seed in mid-spring each year.
EASE OF GROWTH: Easy.
HARVEST TIME AND METHOD: July, or when seed heads are mature. Cut entire stalk, bundle, and hang upside down to air dry.
PREPARATION: Natural; heads may be dyed with floral dip and rinse dyes.
COMMENTS: Keep a close watch on the wheat as it begins to mature, because birds are likely to beat you to it if it is left in the garden too long.

COMMON NAME: Big quaking grass.
LATIN NAME: *Briza maxima.*
CLASSIFICATION: Annual.
COLOR: Golden.

CONDITIONS: Average garden soil.
BEST METHOD: Sow seed directly in the garden in mid-spring.
EASE OF GROWTH: Easy.
HARVEST TIME AND METHOD: Mid-summer or when seed heads mature and turn golden in color. Bundle and hang upside down to air dry.
PREPARATION: Natural.

COMMON NAME: Blue, or Canadian, rye grass.
LATIN NAME: *Elymus canadensis*.
CLASSIFICATION: Perennial to zones 3–8.
COLOR: Blue-green.
CONDITIONS: Average garden soil.
BEST METHOD: Purchase plants with good blue color.
EASE OF GROWTH: Easy.
HARVEST TIME AND METHOD: Late spring or early summer. Cut stems, bundle, and hang upside down to air dry.
PREPARATION: Natural.
COMMENTS: Blue rye grass is highly adaptable and, in most situations, invasive. Plant it by itself—away from other less vigorous garden plants. If over a period of years the grass shows signs of weakening, dig and throw away all but the most vigorous parts of the plant or replace altogether.

COMMON NAME: Broom corn.
LATIN NAME: *Sorghum bicolor*.
CLASSIFICATION: Annual.
COLOR: Tawny, red, or black.
CONDITIONS: Average garden soil.
BEST METHOD: Sow seed mid-spring each year.
EASE OF GROWTH: Easy.
HARVEST TIME AND METHOD: Late summer. Harvest when seeds have formed on the stalks and the color turns golden. Cut entire stalk a foot below where the bloom strands separate from the stem. Allow stalks to dry by standing them upright in a large box. Stalks may be used with or without seed as it remains intact. To remove seed, comb through the strands with a coarse comb.
PREPARATION: Natural.

COMMENTS: This is the grass from which corn brooms are made. Although it is a bit large for most arrangements, this grass is well worth growing.

COMMON NAME: Fountain grass.

LATIN NAME: *Pennisetum* species and cultivars.

CLASSIFICATION: Perennial to zones 6–9.

COLOR: Ivory, golden, or reddish brown.

CONDITIONS: Adaptable, but prefers good garden soil with adequate moisture.

BEST METHOD: Purchase plants, true to name, from a reliable nursery.

EASE OF GROWTH: Easy once established.

HARVEST TIME AND METHOD: Mid- to late summer. Cut stalks, bundle, and hang upside down to air dry.

PREPARATION: Natural.

COMMENTS: Most species are quite tender and for this reason are sometimes grown as annuals in the north. Be certain of what you are buying! For zone 6, *P. alopecuriodes* (but not cultivars of this species), *P. caudatum*, and *P. imcompton* should be hardy.

COMMON NAME: Foxtail millet, Hungarian grass.

LATIN NAME: *Setaria* species.

CLASSIFICATION: Annual.

COLOR: Tawny to red or brown.

CONDITIONS: Average garden soil.

BEST METHOD: Sow seed in mid-spring each year.

EASE OF GROWTH: Easy.

HARVEST TIME AND METHOD: Harvest in mid- to late summer or when seed heads have just matured. Bundle in small bunches and hang upside down to air dry.

PREPARATION: Natural.

COMMON NAME: Hairgrass.

LATIN NAME: *Deschampsia* species.

CLASSIFICATION: Perennial to zones 4–9.

COLOR: Green to golden.

CONDITIONS: Good garden soil with adequate moisture.
BEST METHOD: Purchase plants labeled "true to name" from a reliable nursery.
EASE OF GROWTH: Easy.
HARVEST TIME AND METHOD: Early summer. Cut stems, bundle, and hang upside down to air dry.
PREPARATION: Natural.

COMMON NAME: Hare's tail grass.
LATIN NAME: *Lagurus ovatus*.
CLASSIFICATION: Annual grass.
COLOR: White.
CONDITIONS: Average garden soil and full sun.
BEST METHOD: Sow seeds directly in the garden in mid-spring.
EASE OF GROWTH: Easy.
HARVEST TIME AND METHOD: Early to mid-summer. Cut entire stalk, bundle, and hang upside down to air dry.
PREPARATION: Natural, or may be dyed easily with fabric dye or dip-and-rinse floral dye.

COMMON NAME: Melic grass.
LATIN NAME: *Melica ciliata*.
CLASSIFICATION: Perennial to zones 5–8.
COLOR: Ivory.
CONDITIONS: Fertile well-drained soil and full sun or light shade. Resents dry soil.
BEST METHOD: Purchase plants or sow seed in early spring.
EASE OF GROWTH: Easy.
HARVEST TIME AND METHOD: Early summer. Bundle and hang upside down to air dry.
PREPARATION: Natural.

COMMON NAME: Northern sea oats.
LATIN NAME: *Chasmanthium latifolium*.
CLASSIFICATION: Perennial to zones 5–9.

COLOR: Green, golden, or copper.
CONDITIONS: Rich soil in partial shade.
BEST METHOD: Purchase plants from a reliable nursery.
EASE OF GROWTH: Easy if cultural conditions are met.
HARVEST TIME AND METHOD: Early to late summer. Cut entire stem when flowers develop or turn the color you desire. Bundle and hang upside down to air dry.
PREPARATION: Natural.

COMMON NAME: Pampas grass.
LATIN NAME: *Cortaderia* species.
CLASSIFICATION: Perennial to zones 8–10.
COLOR: White, mauve, or golden.
CONDITIONS: Fertile, well-drained soil.
BEST METHOD: Purchase plants labeled "true to name" from a reliable nursery.
EASE OF GROWTH: Easy once established and given proper growing conditions.
HARVEST TIME AND METHOD: Late summer, or as soon as the flower heads mature. Cut the entire stem and stand upright in a large bucket or box to dry.
PREPARATION: Natural.
COMMENTS: If you choose to plant pampas grass, be sure to choose the right location. Mature clumps can grow to be several feet across and are difficult to move, so plant it where it's going to stay.

COMMON NAME: Perennial quaking grass.
LATIN NAME: *Briza media*.
CLASSIFICATION: Perennial to zones 4–10.
COLOR: Golden.
CONDITIONS: Average garden soil.
BEST METHOD: Sow seed directly in the ground or purchase plants.
EASE OF GROWTH: Easy.
HARVEST TIME AND METHOD: Early summer. Cut seed heads and bundle; hang upside down to air dry.
PREPARATION: Natural.

COMMON NAME: Silver grass.
LATIN NAME: *Miscanthus* species and cultivars.
CLASSIFICATION: Perennial to zones 4 or 5–9.
COLOR: Golden, silver, or red.
CONDITIONS: Good garden soil with good drainage and adequate moisture.
BEST METHOD: Purchase named species and cultivars from a reliable nursery.
EASE OF GROWTH: Easy.
HARVEST TIME AND METHOD: Late summer to early autumn. Cut entire length of stalk and stand upright in a large bucket or box to dry.
PREPARATION: Natural.
COMMENTS: Some *Miscanthus* species can be invasive, especially in light soil. This grass is nearly impossible to dig out, so use caution and plant it away from the garden where it can form a large clump without disturbing other plants.

COMMON NAME: Snowy wood rush.
LATIN NAME: *Luzula nivea*.
CLASSIFICATION: Perennial to zones 4–9.
COLOR: White to ivory.
CONDITIONS: Good garden soil with ample humus and light shade, especially in the south.
BEST METHOD: Purchase plants or sow seed in mid-spring.
EASE OF GROWTH: Easy.
HARVEST TIME AND METHOD: Early summer. Cut entire stalk, bundle, and hang upside down to air dry.
PREPARATION: Natural.
COMMENTS: Snowy wood rush spreads modestly as a ground cover would, so give it ample room in the garden or plant it where it has room to spare.

COMMON NAME: Squirrel's tail grass.
LATIN NAME: *Hordeum jubatum*.
CLASSIFICATION: Perennial to zones 5–9.
COLOR: Medium green.
CONDITIONS: Moist, well-drained soil and full sun.
BEST METHOD: Sow seed in early spring.
EASE OF GROWTH: Easy.

HARVEST TIME AND METHOD: Mid- to late spring. Cut seed heads as soon as they fully develop, as they are frail and, if left too long, will shatter. Bundle and hang upside down to air dry.

PREPARATION: Natural.

COMMENTS: This short-lived perennial can be grown as an annual in an area away from the garden, as any heads not collected will sow voraciously from seed.

Grasses to Collect

Sedges

Sedges, such as *Carex pseudocyperus*, grow wild and are well worth collecting for their interesting flowers. Many are found in ditches or at the edges of ponds. Most sedges bloom in early to mid-summer. Bundle the stalks and hang upside down as you would to dry most grasses.

Cattails

Although we don't think of them as grass, cattails actually belong to that family. There are two types of cattails: large and small. The small cattails are very desirable for smaller arrangements; however, they are also much less common. Harvest cattails as soon as they have fully formed, otherwise they have a tendency to shatter. Dry upright in a large bucket or box. Once they are dry, you may want to spray them with a surface sealer to keep them in top-notch condition.

Reed grass

Reed grass (*Phragmites communis*) is of limited use to the arranger because of its size, but worth mentioning at least. A vigorous and common sight in the northeast, reed grass is a poor substitute for pampas grass, but it is all we have! The color of the plume varies a bit from a fawn color with a purplish cast to a silvery black tint. Harvest reed grass while it is fresh and clean in late summer, and dry stems upright in a large bucket or box.

Pods, Cones, and Other Woody Naturals

PODS

Blackberry lily, poppy, tulip seed heads, and Chinese lanterns.

COMMON NAME: Blackberry lily.
LATIN NAME: *Belamcanda chinensis.*
CLASSIFICATION: Perennial to zone 5.
COLOR: Seed heads are beige with shiny black seeds.
CONDITIONS: Any good garden soil and full sun.
BEST METHOD: Purchase transplants or established plants.
EASE OF GROWTH: Easy.
HARVEST TIME AND METHOD: Mid- to late summer. Cut length of stem, bundle loosely, and hang upside down to air dry.
PREPARATION: Natural.
COMMENTS: This plant looks like an iris, has the name of a lily, and has a seed head that looks like a blackberry—in fact, it is none of the above.

COMMON NAME: Chinese lanterns.
LATIN NAME: *Physalis Alkekengi.*
CLASSIFICATION: Perennial to zone 4.
COLOR: Pods are green, turning bright orange at maturity.
CONDITIONS: Any good garden soil and full sun.
BEST METHOD: Purchase established plants.
EASE OF GROWTH: Easy.
HARVEST TIME AND METHOD: Late summer through fall. Cut stems as the pods turn orange, or earlier if you want them to remain green. Hang stems upside down in loose bundles to air dry or dry on a screen.
PREPARATION: Natural.
COMMENTS: Plant Chinese lanterns well away from the garden, as it will overrun other plants quickly. Protect those pods in storage from rodent damage.

COMMON NAME: Illinois bundle flower.
LATIN NAME: *Desmodium illinoisensis.*
CLASSIFICATION: Perennial to zone 5.
COLOR: Lustrous brown pods.
CONDITIONS: Good garden soil.
BEST METHOD: Purchase plants.
EASE OF GROWTH: Easy.

HARVEST TIME AND METHOD: August through September. Harvest pods on the stem. Store them in plastic bags or containers to prevent rodent damage.

PREPARATION: Natural or gilded.

COMMENTS: This plant is a native American prairie flower.

COMMON NAME: Money plant, honesty.

LATIN NAME: *Lunaria annua.*

CLASSIFICATION: Annual or biennial.

COLOR: Pods are papery white.

CONDITIONS: Average garden soil.

BEST METHOD: Sow seed in mid-spring.

EASE OF GROWTH: Easy.

HARVEST TIME AND METHOD: Early to mid-summer. Pick stems and gather into small bundles. Remove outer husk from each pod. Hang upside down to store.

PREPARATION: Natural.

COMMENTS: A close relative, perennial honesty (*Lunaria redevia*), is rarely offered, but makes a more permanent addition to the garden.

COMMON NAME: Nigella, love-in-a-mist.

LATIN NAME: *Nigella damascena*, *N. orientalis* Transformer.

CLASSIFICATION: Annual.

COLOR: Pods are pale green or pale green and mauve.

CONDITIONS: Good garden soil.

BEST METHOD: Plant seed in early spring, sowing seed heavily. Allow some plants to go to seed at the summer's end each year, and you will always have a bed of nigella.

EASE OF GROWTH: Easy once germinated.

HARVEST TIME AND METHOD: Early to late summer. Only cut the stems of pods that are mature. Bundle and hang upside down to air dry.

PREPARATION: Natural.

COMMENTS: Keep any nigella that you are storing safe from mice and other rodents who would enjoy the seeds in each pod. *N. orientalis* is also a good dried pod.

Common name: Poppy.
Latin name: *Papaver orientale*.
Classification: Perennial to zone 2.
Color: Pods are green to light brown.
Conditions: Any average garden soil that is well drained.
Best method: Purchase first-year, container-grown plants or start from seed.
Ease of growth: Easy once established.
Harvest time and method: Early summer. Cut stems, bundle loosely, and hang upside down to air dry.
Preparation: Natural, or pods may be sprayed with floral paint.
Comments: Various annual poppies may be grown for their pods as well, particularly *Papaver somniferum*. Protect all poppy pods in storage from destruction from rodents.

WOODY NATURALS TO COLLECT

Acorns

Acorns are charming. Whether you are making holiday decorations or just a year-round pine-cone wreath, acorns are a welcome addition. There are many different types of acorns, just as there are cones. If you are lucky enough to be able to collect small bunches of acorns "on the stem" and in small bunches, do take advantage of it.

Bark Curls and Pieces

If you are a hiker, you may have access to an array of barks to add to your arrangements. Do not pass up the opportunity! (But never strip bark off a tree—it is usually fatal to the tree.) Bark texture adds a great deal to natural arrangements. Different types of birch bark are particularly desirable. Large pieces may become the basis for a one-of-a-kind piece, whereas smaller pieces may be able to be worked into a wreath. Keep a small selection on hand to use when the occasion arises.

Birds' Nests

A natural bird's nest can add a realistic touch to an arrangement. They can be collected after the nesting season in your area has passed, and, in fact, are rarely visible until late summer or fall. Small intricate nests make especially nice subjects. Spray birds' nests with a clear high-gloss spray to keep them from shedding excessively.

Pine Cones, Spruce Cones, Fir Cones, Hemlock Cones, etc.

An assortment of pine cones.

Cone is the term we will use to refer to the above listing, unless singling out one cone in particular. After all, unless you are an expert on conifers, you probably will not know the difference between a pine cone and a spruce cone. When you begin to collect them in earnest, however, things change, and you will begin to notice the differences from one cone to another.

Cones are quite valuable to an arranger, if for no other reason than the fact that they last and last. A well-constructed wreath can last a lifetime, literally. The astounding variety of shapes and sizes may surprise you once you start to accumulate them. Collect cones whenever the opportunity arises; a stockpile of many different kinds is like money in the bank to the arranger.

Cotton Pods

The cotton pod has certainly played a large part in American history. It is also a valuable addition to floral arrangements. Cotton pods are widely available in parts of the western and southern United States, where many farmers will allow you to pick the exploding pods if you offer them compensation for their crop. If you are not fortunate enough to find them in the field, try purchasing from a floral supply center.

Fern Fronds

Rather than having spores (seeds) on the backs of their leaves, some ferns produce a woody spore case that is highly ornamental. These decorative fronds are stunning in floral arrangements. They can be left plain, sprayed a color, or gilded with metallic spray paint.

Fern fronds vary in length, from about one foot to more than two feet in length. The most commonly found fronds are those of the sensitive fern (*Onoclea sensibilis*), found throughout the eastern part of the United States. The Ostrich fern (*Matteuccia Struthiopteris*), is less common and is found throughout the northern part of the United States.

Fungi and Lichens

Fungi and lichens may not appeal to everyone, but for others they are irresistible and they certainly are at home on a woodsy wreath, giving it an air of authenticity. Most fungi and lichens are easy to dry—just place them flat on a screen.

When choosing fungi or lichens to dry, it is safest to stay with bracket fungi, a familiar fungi like hen of the woods, or a lichen such as British soldiers. Collecting mushrooms of all types should be off limits, as many can have toxic effects if improperly handled or ingested.

Some fungi and lichens are found growing right into tree branches in the forest. Cut an entire small branch to include in a swag if you can.

Lotus Pods

Lotus pods are the seed cases from certain types of water lilies, found throughout the eastern United States. They are not accessible for most of us to collect, unless you happen to live in an area in which they thrive. The rest of us are resigned to purchasing them from floral supply centers.

Lotus pods are large, and for that reason are often used as the focal point of an arrangement.

Pussy Willows

Pussy willows for many of us are one of the first signs of spring. Because of this and their simple beauty, they are nice to have on hand for spring arrangements particularly.

Pussy willows may be formed into a wreath all by themselves (on a flexible ring form) or may be used in freestanding arrangements. Pick pussy willows just when the fuzzy catkins emerge and are fresh and clean. If you are making a wreath, form it while the pussy willows are green and limber. Otherwise, stand them in a bucket or a box to dry.

Sweet Gum and Sycamore Balls

Depending on the area you live in, sweet gum balls and sycamore balls may be yours to collect. Star-shaped sweet gum balls especially are long-lasting in arrangements, made into a wreath by themselves or mixed into a pine-cone wreath. Sycamore balls are light colored and are also acceptable in any type of woodsy arrangement. Spray sycamore balls with a surface sealer to keep them from exploding.

Teasels

Teasels (*Dipsacus sylvestris*) are the woody seed pod of a native wildflower. This prickly pod has an intriguing shape and form and has always been a favorite of the arranger. Teasels may be used on the stem or may be cut short and placed on large wreaths. They may be stored for many years and can be painted with floral paint in any color you choose. Harvest teasels after they have "hardened" in early autumn.

Topiary Wood

Topiary trunks can be made out of any attractive wood that is available to you. Birch or fruit woods are especially attractive, but trunks can be made out of any wood you find.

To collect and cure wood for topiary, collect fresh wood only—trimmings from trees in your yard will suffice. You will want to match the diameter of the trunk to the size of the topiary, so be prepared and collect pieces of different diameters to have on hand.

Collect unblemished lengths of wood with a straight grain; wood with a slight bend will warp even more once it has dried. Cure the wood in a dry location for several months—three months at least—before you use it. This will allow the wood to dry thoroughly and you can be certain that any piece you use will not warp after the topiary has been made.

Twigs

Twigs are of great value to arrangers. Having said that though, I must tell you that they are devils to work with—usually. Therefore, you may wish to purchase wreath bases formed of twigs, ready to use. There is also an array of other twig forms, ready for the arranger to decorate.

For those bent on trying their hand with twigs, it *can* be done. It is futile to try to identify twigs that might be of use, except perhaps for corkscrew willow twigs. This particular small tree can be grown in most areas of the United States and its twigs twist and turn in the most peculiar way. They are much easier to work with than most—the wood is green and soft and is rather easily plied into the shape you desire—at least until they dry.

Corkscrew willow twigs aside, you must learn to keep your eyes open, and do not be afraid to try something new and different.

Vines

Vines are normally formed into wreath bases and are not generally used otherwise. If you wish to make your own bases, honeysuckle, grape, and hops vines are all satisfactory. A well-formed grapevine wreath can have appeal even in its unadorned state or simply decorated with a few berries and a bow.

4 Odds and Ends in the Natural World

This chapter lists natural items that really do not fit in any of the other categories. Most of them can be collected or can be found at the produce counter. Still others can be grown or can be purchased from a floral supply center. All of the items listed deserve solid consideration when the time comes to stocking your drying shed.

Berries

Depending on what area of the country you live in, you may have a ready supply of berries in your area. While all berries are attractive fresh (such as holly berries at Christmas), those berries that hold on the stem after they have dried are even more desirable.

For most of us, pepperberries, in red or pink, fill the bill and are readily available from floral supply centers. If you like to collect, you can try drying small rose hips (the larger hips are difficult to dry) flat on a screen. As berries contains seeds, it is always wise to protect them adequately from rodents.

Bittersweet

Bittersweet is a berry as well, but worthy of special consideration. These beautiful reminders of fall are actually the fruit of one of two different vines. They can be difficult to collect if they are in the treetops, but are seasonally available from floral supply centers.

Indian Corn

Indian corn is extremely ornamental and is a traditional fall adornment that symbolizes a bountiful harvest. The traditional ear lengths are useful for placing on a door. Miniature Indian corn can also be purchased. These tiny ears are very useful for the tabletop or smaller arrangements and are just as colorful as the larger variety.

Grow Indian corn in the same fashion as sweet or field corn (and protect it from its typical animal admirers), or frequent a local fruit stand and purchase all you need. The husks from this corn are also attractive and are often multi-colored.

Pod Corn

Pod corn is relatively new on the scene. It is a throwback in time to when corn kernels were secreted behind small husks that covered each kernel. Each ear is quite short, so the corn can fit quite nicely into any medium-sized arrangement.

Grow pod corn in the same fashion that you would sweet or field corn. Harvest when inspection of the kernels indicates that they are ripe. You will need to protect this corn from squirrels, raccoons, and the like, just as you would any other corn that you grow.

Feathers

Feathers need to be purchased, unless you are lucky enough to find them on walks. Any type of feather can be used in your choice of arrangements, but the purchased kind make for a more reliable supply. If you like flamboyant feathers, peacock feathers are normally available. Most times pheasant feathers are a good choice because of their moderate size. Even smaller feathers under four inches are available in craft stores. If you know a bird hunter, it can't hurt to inquire as to what they do with the feathers of their conquests.

Fruits and Vegetables

Simple, and always in style, fruits and vegetables can also be used for decorations. Pomegranates, gourds, dried peppers, and okra have all been used as decorations for centuries. Traditionally, fruits and vegetables have been used in fall and winter arrangements.

If you have excellent drying conditions, you may wish to try your hand at drying small peppers and okra. Pomegranates are best left to the professionals to preserve. Gourds should be allowed to dry thoroughly; the skin is then sanded off with a fine sandpaper, and a spray coating of lacquer can be applied to preserve them.

Reindeer Moss

Reindeer moss is at its best in natural arrangements. This sage green moss is one of nature's wonders—when it is dry, it is extremely brittle, but when it is damp, you can walk on it without damaging it in the slightest!

Reindeer moss can sometimes be collected from private property—always ask permission before filling your basket! If you are lucky enough to collect it, or if your purchased moss is untreated, you can preserve its softness by spraying it with a solution of glycerin and water.

Reindeer moss is easier to use if it is treated first with glycerin. Place three tablespoons of vegetable glycerin in a quart spray bottle and fill it to the top with water. Mist the reindeer moss until wet, then allow it to dry out. Repeat this until the moss feels dry, yet soft.

Sheet Moss

Sheet moss is a beautiful decorative moss that has been used for a long time by florists. It can be used to cover a wreath base, the top of a topiary pot, or to form a pretty, natural background.

Sheet moss is best purchased from a floral supply center. Look for a bright green color and a firm, solid mat of moss.

Seashells

Who doesn't like to collect seashells at the shore? Although collecting is not what it used to be, you can still make a beautiful wreath from the shells and creatures that wash up on the beach.

Any type of shell is acceptable for a wreath, and usually they only need to have the seawater washed off. Should you be inclined, as I am, to collect bits and pieces of sea creatures like crabs (or if your shells are a bit rank), you will need to do a bit more work to prepare them for your arrangements. First, soak them overnight in clean water. The next day, place them in a large pan and cover them with water; add a couple of tablespoons of salt to the water. Place on a heat source (the outdoor grill is a great place to do this), and bring the pot to a gentle boil for about twenty minutes. This should cook any remaining animal matter. Remove the shells from the water and allow them to dry thoroughly in the sun—for crab claws and similar items, the drying may take two weeks.

Spices

Star anise and cinnamon sticks are two spices that are attractive enough to place in arrangements. Use star anise on small spice wreaths where you can

Bracken fungus, pod and indian corn, pepperberries, feathers, and shells.

appreciate its unusual shape. Cinnamon sticks, available in a variety of lengths, are more universal and can be used in arrangements large or small; or they can become the base for cinnamon stick bundles, a wonderful holiday decoration.

5 Growing Your Own Special Garden

Raising your own flowers for drying has many rewards. Self-satisfaction, the joy of watching plants grow, economy, and quality are foremost among them.

Once you have made the decision to raise your own flowers, there are several other decisions to be made thereafter. Will I raise plants from seed or buy plants from a grower? How many varieties will I grow and how many of each one? Should I concentrate on annual plants or perennials, and how much space will they take up?

All of these questions and more need to be answered, and the purpose of this chapter is to guide you through the process so that you and your plants have a productive growing season.

PLANTS FROM SEED VERSUS BUYING TRANSPLANTS

The first thing you will need to decide is whether it is better for you to grow your own plants from seed or rely on a local grower from whom you can purchase transplants. Each has advantages and disadvantages, as you will discover.

Raising your own seedlings, or **transplants** as we will refer to them, is an involved proposition, and that is the major disadvantage. You must find a source or sources for the seed, invest in the materials that are necessary to get them started, have a place for them to grow, a light source to grow them with, and a good sunny location for them in the garden. Once these conditions are met, you still need to invest time in sowing, watering, thinning, moving them outdoors, and sometimes transplanting the seedlings. Problematic as they seem, all these terms are most often easily met, with a little determination and juggling of the average household.

For all your trouble, the rewards are highest if you raise your own plants. First and foremost, you will be able to handpick not only the varieties of flowers you want to grow, but the colors you want to grow each in. This is no small achievement when you consider that color is everything when you are faced with making a wreath for your living room.

In visiting the average nursery to buy transplants, you will find precious few dried flowers to choose from, so your flower selection will be hampered from the outset unless you grow your own.

Assuming that you *will* be able to find the flower varieties that you want to grow, color selection at the nursery can be poor. Most growers buy seed in bulk, and unfortunately for us, they are forced to commit large quantities of money to these purchases. The end result is that the growers opt to purchase color mixes in an effort to please some of the buyers, some of the time. Color mixes, in my experience, always fall short of our expectations. Imagine growing your own plants all season, awaiting the blooms. Flower stalks, then buds, appear, but when they open, the flowers are 65 percent yellow instead of the blues and pinks you had hoped for. You will rarely be rewarded with colors in premier shades from a color mixture.

The best way to solve this dilemma is to arm yourself with knowledge and assess your situation as best you can. Study the seed catalogs early enough in the year to allow time to make your decision. Make a list of all the flowers you might want to grow, and become familiar with the color choices for each. When this list is finished, prioritize it! Decide what can possibly be purchased and what you will absolutely need to grow yourself.

Once you have gone this far it should become simple to decide if you have the time and space to grow from seed what you have chosen. Consider how many dozens of each you will want. It is advisable for you to start small, and build on your experience from year to year.

Annuals Versus Perennials

Horticulturalists have divided plants into easily recognized patterns of behavior in an effort to understand them. Plants that grow, flower, set seed, and die in one season are known as annuals. Plants that grow for more than one season before blooming and setting seed, and live for many years, are called perennials. Those that fall in between these two categories are called biennials.

When you are choosing flowers for your garden, it is important to know which flowers are annuals and which are perennials because they will be planted and managed differently in the garden setting. You will need to have a mixture of both annuals and perennials to provide the correct mixture of fillers, primary, and accent flowers for the projects you have in mind.

German statice, Silver King artemisia, and perennial baby's breath are all perennial plants that provide fillers for your arrangements. The mere fact that they will thrive in your garden for year after year should make them attractive to you. After all, these plants do not have to be replaced each season, but will come up reliably where you have planted them. As convenient as this is, you will need to plan garden space for them, taking into consideration their ultimate size, and you may have to wait two years or more for them to bloom to their fullest capacity. Because they only need to be started from seed or purchased once, perennials represent a more stable, onetime investment.

Annuals, on the other hand, need to be replaced each year. They will only produce for one season before the plant is spent. A commitment to growing annuals means that plants will have to be grown or purchased, as well as planted each season, and either way, this is an investment in time or capital.

Some advance planning is advisable for those who endeavor to grow perennials from seed. Each plant responds a bit differently, and some can take up to four years to achieve full bloom. Nonetheless, perennials are the backbone of the flower bed and will reward you for years to come.

Starting Plants from Seed

Starting your plants from seed will require some patience, attention to some small details, and materials that are readily available at a nearby garden center. Unless you are an experienced gardener who has started seedlings in an outdoor setting, it is advisable to begin all but a few plants indoors. This holds true for milder climates as well as colder climates. The reason for this is simple: Germinating seed is easier to do in a controlled environment.

Some seeds are easier than others to get started, even under these controlled conditions. Below you will find my recommendations

Keep a yearly notebook of all the transplants you grow—what colors, how many, and the date the seeds were started. This is a great guide from year to year. You can refer to it if you think that you have been growing too much or not enough of a given flower or color—or it can just refresh your memory and serve as a timetable for you when planting season arrives.

for starting each of the flower seeds listed earlier in the book. As you study the chart, you will find that some of the seeds need special treatment. These treatments help to break the germination code that Mother Nature has set in place. Without these treatments, germination is risky business.

Flower Common Name	Annual/ Perennial/ Biennial	Germination Code	Pack Size	Comments
Helichrysum	A	2	12	*
Statice latifolia	P	3	9	*
Annual statice	A	3	12	* & **
German statice	P	3	9	*
Baby's breath	P	1	12	—
Agastache	P	1	9	***
Lunaria	B	3	—	***
Nigella	A	3	6	—
Sweet Annie	A	1	—	***
Gomphrena	A	4	9	*
Imortelle	A	3	9	—

Germination Codes

1) No special requirements.
2) Soak seed in warm water until they start to sprout.
3) Just cover the seed with a fine dusting of soil; seed may need light to germinate.
4) This seed needs darkness to germinate—cover pack with cardboard and keep in a warm dark place. Check daily for germination.

Comment Code

* Seed germination benefited by 80-degree F temperatures—keep near a heating duct.

** Buy cleaned seed to enhance germination percentage.

*** This seed may be sown in the spot where it is to grow in the garden.

Your flower seedlings should be started eight to twelve weeks in advance of when you would set them into the garden in your area. For us in the north, it means starting usually by mid- to late March at the latest. The shorter your growing season is, the more important it is to start the seeds at the required date. Prolonging the starting date will only delay the harvest, and doing so in areas with short growing seasons cuts the harvest perilously short. If you are unfamiliar with seed-starting dates in your area, consult a local master gardener or growing guide for your region.

After you have the seeds you want in hand, it is time to get started! Below you will find a listing of the items that you will need:

6, 9, or 12 Packs These little growing trays have become popular for do-it-yourselfers in the past few years for good reason. Not only can they be

Potting soil, timer, seeds, labels, and marking pen.

used year after year, but they make moving transplants a breeze. Each one has 6, 9, or 12 individual compartments called cells. The compartments vary slightly in size so that each pack will accommodate a plant of a certain vigor. At transplant time there is no need to cut or otherwise disturb the root system of the plant because it pops right out of its own compartment. These packs are inexpensive and a must for beginners and experienced gardeners alike.

Newspapers These come in handy for plugging the drainage holes in the above packs so that the soil does not run out the holes when the plants are watered. I like to precut them to size then dip them in water so that they stay in place when pushed to the bottom of a cell. Prepare all your packs in advance and you are ready to plant when the mood strikes you!

Seed-Starting Mix This is sometimes called soilless mix and, indeed, some of them contain no actual soil! It is very important to buy the correct mixture for growing seeds indoors. My rule of thumb is that if a bag of growing mix feels heavy when I pick it up, I don't take it home. Seed-starting mix should be light as a feather and you should be able to tell the difference in the store. Don't rely on the manufacturer's description. Heavy soil mixes tend to retain moisture far too long for your seedlings to remain healthy indoors. This invites fungal and disease problems that can kill your best efforts—and your investment—overnight.

Plastic Labels and Indelible Marker It is essential that you label each and every pack that you plant. Although you may think you can rely on memory alone, you will be hard pressed to remember what is what two months down the road! A good investment is an inexpensive package of labels and an indelible nursery marking pen when you order your seeds. Magic markers do not do the trick—nursery marking pens are designed to withstand water and the fading rays of the sun.

Light This is perhaps the most challenging obstacle to overcome when growing seedlings. Unless you are fortunate enough to have a greenhouse or southern-facing sun room in a sunny climate, you will need artificial light to successfully grow seedlings indoors. Despite what you will read in some books and magazines, special light bulbs called **grow bulbs** are not necessary to grow your seedlings. These grow bulbs are expensive to say the least—retailing at twenty dollars a bulb and up! All you really need are fluorescent tubes that cost a dollar each. I like to set up what are commonly called "shop lights," each of which accommodates two four-foot fluorescent tubes. This gives a good amount of light to grow by and for most people one or two of these fixtures set up in the basement is all they will ever need. Be sure to mark the date you put the bulbs into service on the end of the bulb with magic marker. They should be replaced every year to keep them operating economically in regard to the amount of electricity they use.

Growing Table For any one with a basement, this is a simple matter to solve. I like to use a "found" table set up in the basement. The temperature is warm enough for seedlings (55–70 degrees F), and a makeshift table (an old piece of plywood or like item) is no loss when I water and dribble all over the surface. Any corner can be used to grow in as long as lights can be suspended above the growing table.

Timer I grow my plants in the basement and, since I live upstairs, I find a timer invaluable. The small expense of having one will save you from using your lights day after day when you forget to turn them off, and your plants from being in the dark day after day should you forget to turn them on!

SOWING SEED AND CARE OF YOUR SEEDLINGS

Assemble all your materials on a roomy tabletop when you are ready to sow seed. Place paper in the bottom of each cell in the plastic packs you have chosen. Fill each cell to the top with seed-starting mix. The soil is light and airy, and that makes it easy to inhale as you work with it. To avoid this, water the soil down a few days before you plan to work with it. Once each cell is full, tap the soil with another plastic pack until it is firm but not packed in too tightly.

Now you are ready to place the seed in each compartment. It is here that you must follow strictly the recommendations regarding each type of seed. If the seed needs darkness, you must be sure that it is completely covered with soil; if the seed needs light you must fill the cell totally and place the seed gently on top, taking care not to disturb it when you water.

It is a good idea to place more than one seed in each compartment. While most seeds will germinate about 80 percent or more if treated correctly, some will not come up. It is better to be able to thin the seedlings out if you must than to lose precious time by replanting the seed two weeks later.

Once you have planted the seeds, cover them with soil if applicable, and label each pack with a plastic label. Your label should tell the name of the flower as well as the color.

Place the packs in a sink filled with warm or hot water, gently spray the top of the soil with a fine mist from a handheld spray bottle, and let them soak. By spraying the surface of the soil, you speed up the soaking process. When the flats are thoroughly wet, move them to the other side of the sink or place them on several layers of newspaper and let them drain—the newspaper will soak up the extra water. You will want to keep on hand some old nursery trays or cookie sheets to place the flats on because it makes them easier to move around. Place newspaper in the bottom of these and it will keep water from draining out if the packs should still be wet or need to be watered again.

Put the flats in a very warm place, unless your seed requires cool temperatures to germinate. In a week or so you will begin to see signs of germination.

Once your seeds have germinated you have infants in your care. They should be placed under lights immediately. The seedlings will need to be kept warm, say between 55 to 70 degrees F. They will need light about twelve to fourteen hours a day. You should position the light so that it is about three inches from the plants themselves. If foliage touches the bulb, it can burn. Most shop lights have a system that allows the fixture to be moved up and down at will. Should your plants become leggy, you will know that you have moved the light too far away for their liking.

How often to water is a question that is repeatedly asked. The answer is simple: Only your plants know, and it will take observation on your part to get in tune with them. They will tell you if they have had too much or too little. The truth is that they will be unhappy and perhaps die if the soil is too wet. You must allow the soil to dry a bit between waterings, but not let it get so dry that the seedlings die of drought. The fact that small seedlings can dry out quickly because of shallow root systems should have novice growers anxious enough to be checking on their plants daily. Experience will soon dictate how often you need to drench your plants. One item you may wish to invest in if you are going to grow many seedlings is a watering can with a rosette on the head. These rosettes allow only a fine spray of water to flow out of the head. This avoids damage that can be done to small seedlings by the strong jet of water from a regular watering can.

For watering tender seedlings, nothing beats a long-necked watering can. The long neck reaches across a wide table, and the rosette head delivers a gentle spray of water.

After your plants have grown a bit they will be hungry for some nourishment. Remember the seed starter you have used has very little, if any, soil in it and now you will need to feed the seedlings to keep them healthy. The best thing to use for tender young plants is liquid kelp at regular strength. If you cannot find this product, use any of the commercial houseplant fertilizers at half their recommended strength. You will need to fertilize once a week until your transplants go into the garden.

MOVING YOUR TRANSPLANTS INTO THE GREAT OUTDOORS

It is a beautiful spring day! It is time for your transplants to begin the transition from their protected growing area indoors to the real world outside. This is easily accomplished if you take care to follow a few commonsense tips.

For the last two months or so, your plants have been growing in a protected environment. There has been no wind, no sun, and no pelting rain for them to contend with. While this may seem good on the surface, it has actually left your seedlings weak in the knees. It is now your job to help them adjust gradually to the outdoor environs where they will grow. In doing this you will be creating healthy, strong transplants that will make the transition into your garden with ease.

This process is called hardening off. The best place to accomplish this is in a semiprotected place, such as a **cold frame.** A cold frame is a seasonal compromise between a greenhouse and the outdoors. In a cold frame, your plants will feel the effects of the sun, wind, and rain in moderation. This will eventually strengthen the plants until they will need no protection at all.

There are some important things to consider before your transplants make their move: watering, the effects of the sun, and cold temperatures.

How will they be watered? Because evaporation takes place much more quickly outdoors, you will need to water them much more often, perhaps once a day or more, depending on the exact conditions. You will not be able to water them with a strong blast from a hose, but they should not be coddled, either. They will strengthen faster if they are watered with a moderately strong spray of water.

Also consider the bleaching effect of the sun. Although your seedlings have been under light, the sun is much more powerful. They can be burned or killed by the sun if they are left unprotected for just a couple of hours. A screen just like the one we use in screen doors is a perfect protector for your tender transplants. Leave it on at first all day, then begin removing it in the morning for an hour or two. In cloudy weather you can remove it altogether. Gradually your transplants will be able to be left unprotected for longer periods of time. When they reach this point, it is time to expose them to the midday sun for just a few minutes at first. Always check for bleaching, and take it slow, as the noon sun is the strongest, and damage can occur in minutes. Soon your transplants will be able to withstand the full effects of the sun all day.

If you have a cold frame that has a fitted cover, you are prepared for cold temperatures at night. If frost threatens, or even if it gets unseasonably cold, you should put the cover into operation to protect the transplants. They will stay snugly warm in all but the coldest weather until things warm up outside.

If you do not have a cold frame to help make the transition from indoors to outdoors, controlling these conditions will be a bit more difficult, but it is possible. You may have to use the shade of a tree to protect from the sun, and you may have to haul your tender transplants into the house, garage, or porch if a cold snap threatens. The important thing is to make each move toward the garden gradually.

CREATING THE GARDEN PLAN

When you consider the plan for growing flowers you must first think about what you will need to create wreaths, topiaries, and other pieces. Few people realize that there is, or at least should be, some rhyme or reason to what you grow and how much of each item you grow other than planting your personal favorites.

If you think about a wreath and look at real examples, this theory will become crystal clear. The main portion of any given wreath is the filler. A filler is background material on which you can artfully display primary and accent flowers to their best advantage. You will need far more filler than you will primary flowers, and you will need more primary flowers than accent flowers, and so on. Once you have established this order in your mind, it is a simple thing to sit down and choose from the flowers available by seed or plants.

If there is one thing that is always underestimated, it is the amount of filler needed to finish a wreath or other piece. My students express great surprise when they see me carting trunkloads of baby's breath or German statice to class for them to work with. My nightmare will always be running short of fillers. You can never have too much of them and can always find a use for any that are left over.

Decide what fillers you would like, then decide on primary and accent flowers. Always take into consideration the items that can be collected in wild places. Again, the biggest sin is to run short of filler—you will need tons of the stuff, and it always commands a premium price when you go to purchase it.

Below are some garden plans that incorporate fillers and primary and accent flowers into their design. You will note that the gardens are necessarily heavy on fillers. Their shortcoming is that, with few exceptions, plants that provide fillers are only able to be harvested once a season. Most people would do well when adapting these plans for their own use to count on 75 percent of the designated space for growing fillers.

Adapting Wild Plants into the Garden Plan

I love wild plants, especially those that provide a flower or seed head that I like to arrange with. Wild plants that provide such things are easy to come by in rural—and even urban—locations. The one thing that you can never really count on, though, is accessibility. That favorite lot you have been eyeing for its teasels may be developed by fall, or someone else may beat you to them! Another downfall may be finding the time to make the expedition to collect what you are after.

It is for these reasons that I like to incorporate wild plants into my garden. When making plans to bring a "wild one" home, you must think about ultimately how much you will want to have on hand. As few fillers grow wild, you will usually need only a moderate amount of whatever you have your eye on.

If I only need a bit, and the plant is a perennial, I am inclined to collect a few, or some seed, and include the plant in my cottage garden alongside

Sample Garden Layout 1

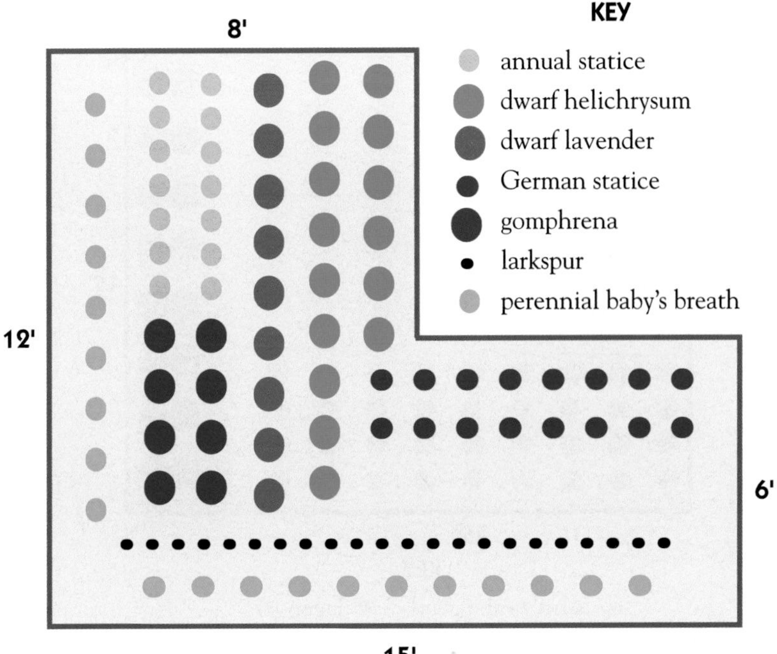

Sample Garden Layout 2

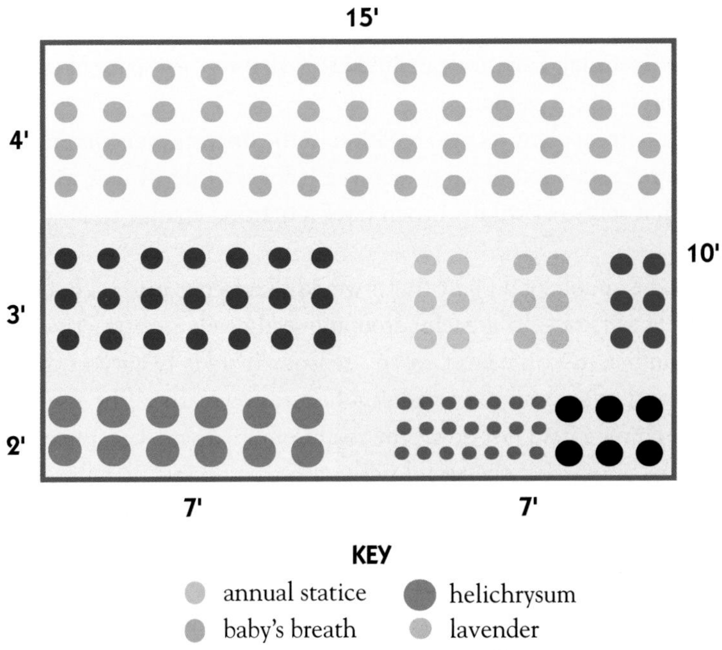

SAMPLE GARDEN LAYOUT 3

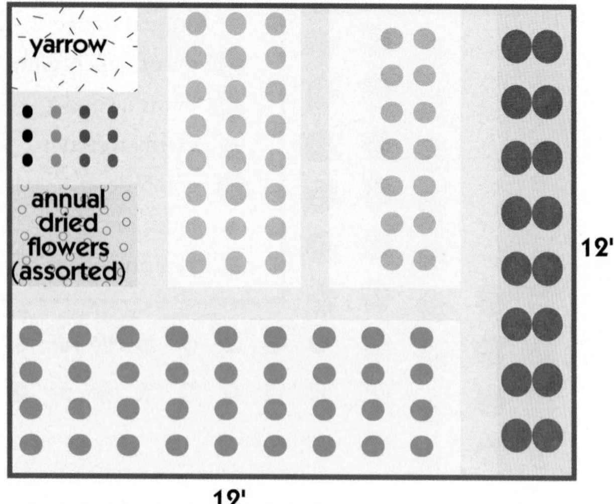

KEY

- achillea the pearl
- art. stellerana
- baby's breath
- German statice
- lavender
- sage
- santolina
- Silver King artemisia

herbs and other perennials. If I am lusting after quantity, or if the plant is an annual or biennial, I am more inclined to give it its own space alongside the other flowers in the garden.

When I give a plant its own location in the dried-flower garden, it sometimes serves as a good place to observe it for a while. If it is weedy or an annual that self-sows wildly, I then have a fighting chance to keep it under wraps.

A good example of a plant that I would like to put into such a situation is squirrel's tail grass. Its graceful drooping seed heads are attractive green or golden amber in color later in the season. It adds beauty and grace to wreaths and swags and even makes a beautiful wreath all by itself. I have been watching a field just down the road from my home because it is full of the desired grass. It is a beautiful sight with the sun setting behind it, but I know it must be invasive because it is the dominant plant in this five-acre or larger field! I suggest moving slowly and with caution with such a plant, or soon it will be invading your potted houseplants. I plan to collect some seed this spring and sow it in a secluded place near the back of the garden—but if I did not have such a secluded place I would just leave it where it is for fear of what it might do if it were to escape!

The Harvest

METHODS OF DRYING THE HARVEST

Many of you will be familiar with the methods used to dry flowers, but there can still be misconceptions on just how to go about it. I have looked at many volumes that give suggestions for methods that may work for someone with unlimited time, budget, and access to professional equipment, but not for a hobbyist working at home. In this chapter I will discuss just what I feel is practical for you to tackle at home—and what is not.

There are only a few ways of drying flowers that need concern you: air drying hanging bundles, air drying flowers upright, drying flowers flat on a screen, and drying in silica gel. To find the best method of drying a given flower, check the individual listings or the chart later in this section. There is no mystery or secret about any of these methods, so let's discuss each one individually.

Air Drying Hanging Bundles

Air drying bundles is one of the best methods used to dry flowers. One advantage includes bundling many stems together and hanging the bundles overhead—thereby saving space. Time is also saved by not having to give each flower individual attention. Finally, air is free to circulate all around the flowers, drying them thoroughly.

Air drying bundles has another advantage in that not many materials are needed to complete the task. All that is needed is a drying line, rubber-

bands, and clothespins. Simply wrap the rubberbands tightly around the stems of each bundle and hang them upside down on the line like you would if you were hanging clothes. Take care to keep the bundles small enough so that their size does not impair the flower's ability to dry.

Drying Materials Upright

Drying upright is as simple as hanging bundles to dry—maybe even simpler. I use this method for items that are difficult to handle because of their overall size or the size of the flower heads. Cattails and Silver King are examples of plants I would dry in this fashion.

All that is needed is a small number of five-gallon buckets or large boxes. When the material is harvested, remove all extraneous foliage (especially any that is to be placed in the bucket) that may impair the drying process. Place the material loosely in the container, and allow it to dry thoroughly.

Drying Flowers Flat on a Screen

Many flowers are quite happy to be dried flat on a screen, which allows air to circulate over and under the flower heads. I have found this method to

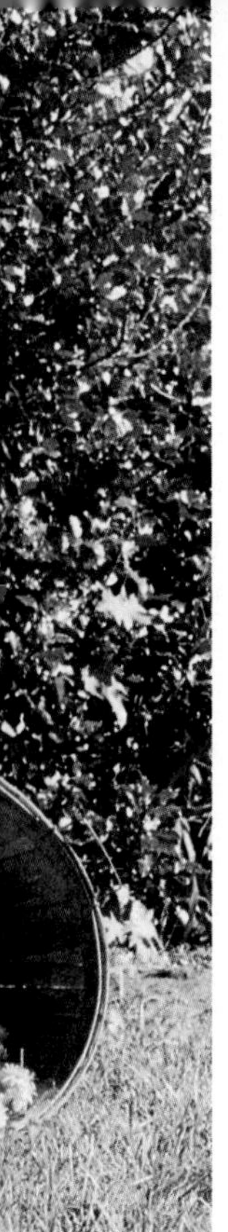

be as versatile as hanging bunches to dry. All that is needed is a screen, especially made or improvised (old window screens work well and are sometimes free for the taking).

After harvesting, simply lay the flowers in a single layer on the screen. Allow the proper length of time for complete drying, and then, if space is at a premium, remove the dry flowers to boxes or bags for storage. If space is not a problem the flowers can remain on the screen indefinitely.

Drying in Silica Gel

Drying flowers in silica gel is the "fussiest" method of drying flowers for the hobbyist; great care must be taken when placing the flowers and the drying takes a good amount of time. It is not my method of choice, and may not be yours, but it may come in handy to dry a flower you feel you just cannot live without. I know folks that swear by it and have excellent results using this method.

Silica gel is fairly expensive. Folks who use it usually buy a small amount and reuse it. Once it has taken on too much moisture to properly dry the flowers, it can be dried slowly in the oven and then is ready to use all over again.

If you are on a budget, you may want to try an alternative material first. Sand, borax, and cornmeal have all been used as substitutes for silica. Some

Drying screen.

swear by these substitutes, and others claim that each one has its faults, such as leaving dents in the flower petals. Only experience will determine which one you prefer.

These mediums are usually used for drying fleshy flowers—in other words, flowers that normally do not dry well at all. Trial and error will tell you which flowers you will want to dry this way.

To dry flowers with any of the above materials, you need a plastic container with a snap-on lid (shoe-box size is good to work with) and the drying medium of your choice. Layer the medium across the bottom to a depth of one inch—more if you are drying large flowers. Place the flowers facedown in the medium, continue until you have one layer, then sift the drying medium over the flowers gently until all parts are covered. Add more medium for the next layer of flowers and continue until the container is full.

Most flowers will dry within a week or ten days using this method. Some colors do fade or change using this method. Check the top layer and when dry, gently pour out the medium, collecting the flowers as you go. Occasionally flowers that are dried this way need to have the drying medium brushed off with a paint brush in order to look their best.

DRYING FLOWERS

Flower Name	Air Bundles	Screen	Upright
Anise hyssop	X	X	
Annual statice	X		
Baby's breath	X		
Cockscomb	X	X	
German statice	X		
Globe thistle	X		
Gomphrena		X	
Hydrangea	X	X	
Helichrysum		X	
Pearly everlasting		X	
Rose	X		
Sea holly	X		
Silver King	X		X
Statice latifolia	X		
Sunflower	X		
Sweet Annie	X		X
Tansy	X		
Yarrow	X		

This chart does not include silica drying, as this method is usually only used for flowers that are not standard dried material.

Creating a Drying Space

is is a good use of drying space. Baby's breath dries ight on a pallet and Silver King hangs directly overhead.

Creating a drying space is easy if you have a bit of space to work with. There are only two important prerequisites for a drying space: It must be dry and dark. Once you have these two requirements satisfied, the rest is easy.

Look for a space where you have floor to ceiling available. Darkness, or the ability to create darkness (I painted the windows of our drying shed) is a must because too many flowers are faded by natural light infiltration. You may have to choose a spot in your basement, in which case it may not be dry, but you can always rely on a dehumidifier to remedy that problem. Whatever space you choose, it should be yours alone; at times you will be making a mess of it and you will need to manage your inventory, no matter how large or how small. If you are unable to create a space that is dark, you may want to consider drying your flowers and then removing them to a dark storage area to protect them from damaging light.

Once you have chosen a space to call your own, you need to create drying lines for air drying. These lines should be about eighteen to twenty-four inches from each other to allow for headroom and the width of some items you will be drying, such as German statice. Do not neglect the ability to string vertical drying lines as well as horizontal ones.

Another must for your drying space is screens, and you should handle them in the most economical and space-saving way possible. I was offered an old lumber drying rack; we fitted it with screens and it has been wonderful. If you have little space you may wish to accommodate smaller screens along a wall under your drying lines—supporting them like you would

Drying lines should be well spaced to ensure that you can move freely between them and to promote good air circulation.

shelving and attaching the brackets on which they lay directly to the wall. Floor space can easily be used for drying materials upright.

Drying screens can be used for a variety of natural materials. Once completely dry, flowers can be stored in plastic bags to free up space for drying a new crop.

Take your time and work with an idea before you implement it. A well-designed space is worth its weight in gold. Storage boxes or perhaps an old dresser can hold hardware and act as an organizer for greening pins, wreath bases, glue sticks, floral picks, and other tools of the trade.

If you have the luxury of space, and an electrical outlet is accessible, you may wish to incorporate a work space where you can create your arrangements—it's handy to have everything close at hand at the moment of creation.

HARVEST TIME

It is exciting at harvest time to see the fruits of your labors materialize and begin to pile up in your drying space. Perennials such as baby's breath and statice have their own harvest time, separate from annual crops. When they are at their peak, there is no time to waste in getting them processed. Pick and process them promptly.

Once the harvest of annuals begins, you can expect to harvest at least once a week, depending on your climate. Unless you have a huge planting, harvesting and processing should not take up all that much time, but it does need to be done on a schedule. Keep a watchful eye on your flowers to learn how quickly they can be harvested after the first picking. The sooner you pick them again (without rushing them), the sooner they will be making more flowers for you to harvest.

Never pick plant material when it is wet. The best time to pick is in the morning after the dew has evaporated from the plants. Once your flowers have been picked, do not delay in processing them. They will be at their best if you process them the same day they are picked.

MANAGING YOUR INVENTORY AND MAINTAINING QUALITY

All flowers have a different shelf life. Some, like helichrysum, last for several years with little care. Gomphrena, on the other hand, fades rather quickly. Some flowers deteriorate only because they are more fragile than others. Time and experience will tell you how long you can depend on a particular crop to last.

Some flowers can be protected from fading by boxing or bagging them for storage after they have dried. Be certain that any material you store in this way is totally dry before it goes into storage, or mildew and mold are likely to render them useless. This method of storage is also a good way to deter mice from attacking their favorite foods in your storage area. I always have to protect nigella and gomphrena especially.

As you use the flowers you have grown, you will get a better feel for how many you need and how far they go in arrangements. Keep your drying area from becoming unmanageable by using older inventories of flowers first, not overgrowing a particular crop from year to year, and discarding flowers too far gone to dye or otherwise use.

Insect Damage

Occasionally insects will invade your dried materials, eating their way through quite a few flowers before you realize what is happening. It is hard to pinpoint what insects might be a problem throughout the country, but there are a lot of them potentially. One rule of thumb is that if you observe unusual insect activity, investigate to be on the safe side.

Indian meal moth is a widespread pest that can do a lot of damage. It is the same moth that invades cornmeal and flours. Pheromone traps sold at kitchen supply houses keep the pest at bay. They are an inexpensive insurance policy against a potentially large problem.

Part 2

Tools and Techniques

7 The Arranger's Tool Chest

Today's arranger is lucky indeed. When I began to teach myself the art of arranging, glue guns hadn't been invented. Things sure have come a long way in a few short years. Today, nearly anything is possible.

There are some basic items that are indispensable for making arrangements. In this chapter I will introduce you to them. Most are reasonably priced and widely available in stores across the country. These are the items you cannot live without. When you purchase tools, it pays to buy quality. It will make your hobby more enjoyable.

GLUE GUNS AND HOT MELT GLUES

Glue guns are one of the most wide-reaching innovations in the craft market of the last several years. They enable a lot of things to be done that otherwise would be difficult at best.

There are several types of glue guns on the market. The major differences between glue guns are the size of the gun, the temperature of the gun ("hot melt" or "low temp"), and whether or not the gun has a trigger to help speed the glue on its way. Although these features are mostly personal preference, I do have some recommendations.

The size of the gun you use is not that important unless you envision yourself using it a lot. If you have never used a glue gun before, don't underestimate the amount of time it will spend by your side while you are plying your crafts. Many women buy a small gun because they feel it will fit their

Glue gun, sticks, greening pins, picks, and floral tape.

hand better or they will be able to control it better. I have very small hands and can say that a large glue gun is easy for me to handle. Also, if you are working for an afternoon, replacing those small glue sticks every two minutes can become annoying. I have had students try their small guns on pine cones when making a wreath, and sometimes an entire stick of that size is not enough to glue on a large cone. If you can afford a medium-priced large glue gun, I would recommend it for your tool chest.

Although tempting for those of us who have burned ourselves with the hot melt guns, low temp guns are for children. The glue sets up so fast that it leaves no time for you to think about what you are doing, or change your mind for that matter. As the glue starts to set, you also get poorer adhesion with a low temp gun. Buy a hot melt and give it the respect it deserves.

As for triggerless guns, I do not understand why they are made! Never buy a glue gun without a trigger: The glue is just too difficult to dispense without one.

GLUE POTS

Glue pots work on the same principle as a glue gun. The pot of glue comes in especially handy though, if you're working with a lot of items that can be dipped in glue to save a little time. Be sure you know what type of glue your pot is designed for before you buy, and be sure that the glue will be readily available for you to purchase.

FLORAL SPRAYS

Many brands of special spray paints are on the market and are touted as floral sprays. What makes them different from other spray paints? Color selection.

Usually the pastels or trendy colors we seek are not available except in expensive floral spray paints. The difference in price can be as much as four to five dollars a can, so it pays to shop around. In my area I have been able to find a line of regular spray paints that have nearly every color I desire, including pastels and country colors. When the rare occasion occurs that I want a color I am unable to find, I pay the price for floral spray paint, knowing that I have saved myself a bundle on other colors in the past.

Aside from pastels and trendy colors, metallic spray paints are useful. Also available are sprays that give a mother-of-pearl sheen to some items; they are available at craft or floral supply centers.

DYES

Floral dyes are not as available as other items discussed in this chapter. Floral dyes usually have instructions to "dip and rinse" the flowers—meaning you dip the flowers in the dye, and rinse them under cold water. This type of dye is quite concentrated, usually is alcohol-based, and makes vibrant, not-so-natural colors.

A better alternative for dying flowers at home are regular fabric dyes. Almost any color is available to you, and the colors you can achieve are softer and more natural-looking. The dying process (discussed in detail in chapter 8) is easy to do at home.

FLORAL PICKS

Floral picks are thin, pointed pieces of wood. They have a thin piece of wire attached to the top end and they are usually dyed an inconspicuous dark green color. Floral picks are standard equipment and are used to make short-stemmed flowers usable by providing them with a larger stem. The wire is wrapped tightly around the flowers and the pick is inserted into the floral foam in place of a natural stem. For instructions on using floral picks, see page 78.

FLORAL TAPE AND CORSAGE TAPE

Floral tape and corsage tape come in very handy at times. This special tape-like material becomes sticky on both sides when it is stretched, then can be wound around whatever you are working on to give a little additional support.

Floral tape is dark green, so it is not easily seen in an arrangement. Corsage tape is white and blends in better when you are working on an arrangement like a tussie-mussie.

A roll or two of each will last a long time for most arrangers.

FLORAL FOAM/STYROFOAM

Floral foam is most useful when making centerpieces, swags, unusually shaped pieces, and live arrangements.

There are two types of floral foam on the market. The first type is green and is sold under the trade name Oasis. This type of foam is used for fresh floral arrangements. It is valued because of its ability to soak up many times its weight in water, thus sustaining fresh arrangements.

The second type of foam is usually a light brown color and is aptly sold under the trade name Sahara. This type of foam holds up under the woody stems often used in dried arrangements, without allowing the stems to move once they are in position.

Both of these foams are sold in bricks. These bricks are easily cut into smaller pieces so that they can be utilized in arrangements.

Styrofoam is also used in arrangements. The most common use for this material is for the head of a topiary. I do not recommend it for wreath bases—there are other more worthy materials to work with.

DESIGN BOWLS

Design bowls are primarily used for fresh flower arrangements or for centerpieces. They are made of lightweight plastic and have fingers built into the bottom of the bowl to hold the floral foam securely in place. They are usually available in white or dark green and can be used for both fresh and dried arrangements.

READY-MADE WREATH BASES

There are several types of wreath bases available today. Straw bases, Spanish moss bases, wire bases (single, double, or crimp-style), twig wreath bases, and vine wreath bases are all widely available.

Crimp-ring form, oasis foam wreath base, styroball, straw base, and Spanish moss base.

Straw wreath bases have been popular for years. Most people use straw wreaths as a base on which to attach baby's breath, foliage, or another filler to create a wreath. Greening pins, or fern pins as they are sometimes called, are used to hold the filler securely to the base. This is accomplished by first pinning the material on the inside of the wreath, then the top, and finally to the outer surface of the wreath (see chapter 8). This is a very effective way of making a wreath if you want to make a large and impressive one and have a lot of material to work with.

Spanish moss bases are very handy. As opposed to straw, which is quite bulky, Spanish moss can be shaped to create small, more delicate wreaths (see chapter 8). Because Spanish moss is very decorative itself, every square inch of the base need not be covered with filler or flowers. This makes a more economical use of your harvest, without sacrificing the appearance of the wreath.

Wire wreath forms are also very versatile. Single-wire forms or double-wire forms can be used to handwire fillers to create a beautiful background for a wreath. Crimp-wire forms negate the need to handwire materials onto the form and make a quick and easy wreath. (For more on wire wreath forms, see chapter 8.)

Twig wreath bases and vine wreath bases are also very popular today. They come in any number of shapes and sizes and often need very little decoration in order to make a lovely wreath. Vine bases are so inexpensive that making your own is not necessary. Twig bases are more expensive, but making them at home can be so difficult that most craft people are resigned to buying them.

Greening, or Fern, Pins

Greening pins are so called because they are used to attach the greens to the bases of wreaths. Often the greens were ferns, hence their other name.

Greening pins are used primarily on straw bases. They are shaped like an exaggerated staple with sharp ends. Some elbow grease is required to push them into a straw base. Greening pins are sold in five-pound boxes or small packages.

8 Techniques You Should Know

When the time comes to put together a floral arrangement for the first time, there is much to learn. While some techniques can be executed reasonably well the first time through, others take a great deal of time. Some of these tasks will come easily to you, and others will always be difficult to do well. In this chapter are many such tasks, some of which are preliminary.

I have placed these tasks apart from the design instructions for two reasons. The first is to simplify the actual design instructions in Part Three of this book. Those instructions will constantly refer you back to this section; for example, when handwiring a wreath base. The second reason for segregating these instructions is that each task will be easier to find should you decide to make a floral design that is not in this book or simply to practice.

Remember, practice does make perfect, and the ultimate goal is for you to become confident enough to design your own floral pieces.

DYING FLOWERS AND FOLIAGE

The task of dying flowers or foliage, I admit, does not sound exciting, but it is a very useful thing to know. You can give new life to unusable flowers and foliages that are far too faded to otherwise use. To some this may sound a bit chintzy, but there is absolutely nothing wrong with this practice. You have already invested time, money, and labor into growing or collecting the item in question; why should it be thrown away if it still has some life left in it? Another consideration is that certain colors are just not to be had in the natural world of dried flowers. Dying flowers in the desired shade allows you to cheat Mother Nature—just this once.

Experience will teach you a lot about which flowers will take dye and which will not. I have included a general chart of flowers that dye well to use as a general reference.

DYING FLOWERS*

FLOWER NAME	FABRIC DYE	DIP-AND-RINSE DYE
Annual statice		X
Field yarrow	X	X
German statice	X	X
Gomphrena	X	
Hydrangea	X	
Pearly everlasting	X	X
Santolina	X	X
Tansy	X	
Yarrow	X	

*Flowers that do not dye well include helichrysum and immortelle.

There are two types of dye that I have found suitable for using on dried flowers. Standard fabric dye, commonly available in a powdered or liquid form, works quite well. Another option is to use floral "dip and rinse" dyes. These dyes are alcohol-based, and they may not be as cost-effective as the standard fabric dyes.

Dying Flowers and Foliage with Fabric Dye

I find the following the best overall method to use when dying dried flowers. It is economical and easy to do, a wide range of colors are available to choose from, and the flowers are quite fade-resistant. Follow the steps below for good results every time. Because the dye tends to stain some pots, pans, and utensils, you may want to designate a less valuable pot as your dye pot. Be sure to wear old clothing when doing this project.

MATERIALS

- *saucepan*
- *fabric dye of your choice*
- *stove or hot plate*
- *slotted spoon*
- *colander*
- *stainless steel or glass bowl*
- *newspapers*

1. Place the flowers to be dyed in a saucepan. Be sure to use a fairly large pot—the flowers will need to simmer for a bit, and the dye will bubble up the sides of the pan.

2. You may use liquid dye or powdered dye. I find the liquid to be very convenient. Place water in the pot to just cover the flowers. Pour in several tablespoons of liquid dye. If you are trying to get a light color, use less dye—sometimes overdoing it will result in a darker color than you would like. You can always add more dye if the color does not come out as dark as you would like.

3. Set the saucepan on a burner and turn the burner on a medium setting. Do not leave the pot unattended at any time, as the dye water will make quite a mess if it spills over the sides. Allow the water to come to a gentle simmering boil. Press down the flowers with the back of a slotted spoon gently, making sure that all the flowers are covered with the dye mixture.

4. Five minutes of this gentle simmer is all it should take for the flowers to take on the color you desire. If they are not dark enough to suit you at this point, add a little bit more dye and repeat the process.

5. When the flowers are the color you desire, remove the pan from the heat. Place a colander over a bowl and spoon in the flowers so that they may drip-dry a bit. The dye water can be reused at a later date, or you may dispose of it if you wish. If you use your sink, be sure to clean it with a bleaching cleanser immediately to remove any stains.

6. Remove the flowers from the colander and place them on newspaper to dry.

Dying Flowers and Foliage with Floral Dye

Another way to dye flowers and foliage is with floral or "dip and rinse" dye. These alcohol-based dyes are sold at floral-supply or craft stores. Each manufacturer places complete instructions on using the dye right on the container. Generally, the flowers are dipped in the dye, which dyes them immediately. The flowers are then rinsed with clear water and allowed to dry.

I find several disadvantages to using these types of dye: They are quite a bit more expensive than fabric dyes, suppliers seem to carry only a small range of colors, some of the colors are quite unnatural-looking, and some of the dyed colors (such as red) tend to fade quickly.

FORMING FLOWER BUNDLES

Forming flower bundles sounds easy enough, right? Well, it is easy, but still takes a bit of practice to perfect. The way you form your bundles when creating a wreath, for example, can make all the difference in the world. Your bundles should be geared to the piece you are making; for example, loose airy bundles for crimp-ring wreath forms and tight compact bundles for handwired wreaths.

The material you are working with will also make a big difference. Working with baby's breath is very different from working with German statice. Again, practice makes perfect. Below are some general guidelines for you to follow.

Gathering a bunch of flowers.

1. Break up your flower stems into nearly even lengths. Make a pile of stems from which you can work. Always leave stems longer than you think you might need—you can always cut them later, but you can never add length once it is gone.

2. Place several stems together, adding them one at a time. Break or cut the stems as much as needed to make an even bundle. Keep the flower tops even—if they are uneven, your arrangement will not look as proportioned as you want it to. If it becomes muddled-looking—with too many flowers in the center—your stems are probably too long and you are forcing too many flowers together as a result. If this happens, disassemble the bundle and start over. Continue adding stems until the bundle is the size required for the wreath that you are making.

3. Keep all your bundles approximately the same size. While Mother Nature is not perfect, too much variation from one bundle to the next will make your arrangement uneven.

4. Keep in mind the size and type of arrangement you are working on. Handwired wreaths, for example, require full, tight, uniform bundles. Bundles for other arrangements may look better if left more loose and airy in appearance.

USING FLORAL PICKS

Floral picks are short pieces of wood with a point on one end and wire attached to the other. They take the place of a stem when the flowers you are working with have little stem, or give the material a more rigid stem so that it may be solidly placed in floral foam.

Floral picks are dyed dark green and are most commonly used in centerpieces and other arrangements that are made on floral foam. Floral picks are available in a number of sizes, most commonly three to six inches in

Making a flower bundle.

length. Choose the size that is appropriate for the arrangement you are working on.

The easiest way to use picks is to gather your material first into the desired shape. Place the stem against the pick, keeping the wire just below the "head" of the flower or foliage. Wrap the wire tightly around the stem. You may wrap the stem and pick with floral tape for added strength if you desire.

USING A GLUE GUN

Glue guns are one of the most valuable tools for today's arranger. They make a lot of things possible that were unthinkable just a few short years ago.

Using a glue gun takes little practice, but using one without making a mess is challenging. Below are some additional items and a few tricks that make using a glue gun a bit cleaner.

- Always keep with your glue gun a disposable pie plate. Use this to set your gun on when it is not in your hand. If it leaks glue, no harm will be done. If you use your gun like I do (often and always in the same location), you may want a heavier tray on which to set it. I use an old enamel tray, and when it gets loaded with glue I set it on a burner on the stove to loosen the excess glue so that I can remove it.
- If you use a hot melt gun, always be careful not to burn yourself—you will, of course, but you need to minimize the risk. If you work sitting down, make sure that your legs are covered. I learned this the hard way (wearing shorts) when a piece I was working on catapulted a huge mass of hot glue onto my bare leg. I got to peel it off my burned skin after it hardened. When you work with small flowers that are hard to keep a grip on, use a pair of regular or long-handled tweezers to spare your fingertips. If you are prone to burning yourself a lot, keep a pan of ice water nearby, and invest in an aloe vera plant to salve your wounds.
- Avoiding "cobwebs" should be done at all cost. These annoying leftover strands of glue will cloud the beauty of your arrangement and will take forever to pick off. Try this method: Apply glue to the surface of a flower. Before you remove the tip of the gun, twirl the gun in a circular motion. This action will cut the string off and save you a lot of work.
- When working with large, heavy pieces such as pine cones, do not spare the glue. Heavy objects take a lot of glue if they are to be held in place forever. If you do a lot of work with such items, you will need a large hot melt gun.

WORKING WITH FLORAL FOAM

There are two or three types of foam used in the floral trade. Oasis, Sahara, and regular Styrofoam are all commonly used. For descriptions of these foams, see page 71.

All three of these items are similar to work with. Glue will not adhere well to any of these foams except Styrofoam. If you are using hot melt glue on Styrofoam, it will eat away at the foam; a better choice is a low-temperature glue or a standard white craft glue. If you must use a high-temperature glue gun, use it just after it has been plugged in. The tendency to eat away the Styrofoam will be lessened because the glue will not be as hot.

Usually when you use foam to create an arrangement, the floral stems are placed in the foam. I know from teaching experience that this task takes some getting used to. The tendency is to always push the material too far into the foam. In fact, you need only place the material in about one-half inch in order to get it to stay in place.

CONSTRUCTING A WREATH BASE

If you are economically minded, or like to work with odd shapes and sizes, knowing how to make your own wreath bases comes in very handy.

Wreath bases can be made from several different materials. Spanish moss, wire, and even cardboard can be used to good effect. Just which type of base you choose will be influenced by the materials at hand and the type of wreath you are going to make.

Below you will find instructions and suggestions for constructing and using each type of base.

Making a Wire-Form Base

Knowing how to make a wire-form base is very useful. This wire form is the backbone and strength of the wreath that will eventually be created around it. Knowing how to make this type of form will allow you to make nearly any size or shape wreath you want and is useful for making handwired wreaths or Spanish moss bases. Wire forms can also be used as a guide for making vine bases.

Starting with the right type of wire is very important. In my experience most hardware stores do not carry the gauge wire you will need for this task. I have had the best luck at a farm store where I can find fencing wire in the correct gauge. Start with 14-gauge wire, and follow the instructions.

MATERIALS

- *paper*
- *pencil*
- *string*
- *14-gauge wire*
- *heavy-duty wire cutters*
- *needle-nose pliers*
- *floral tape*

1. Decide the size and shape of the wreath you want to create. If the material used will extend beyond the wire-form base, approximate how far it will extend, take that into account, and deduct that from the finished size of the wreath. This should leave you with the size of the wire form you must make.

2. Draw out on a piece of paper the outline of the wreath. Use a piece of string to measure all around the outline. Measure the length of string, add six inches to this measurement, and cut the wire to this length using the wire cutters. This is the amount of wire you will need to cut in order to make the wire base. Keep a record of these measurements on hand for the next time you are making a base of that size.

3. Draw the wire together, making the wire shape the size you have chosen. Overlap the wire at the top, crisscrossing the wire and wrapping one end around to prevent the wire from slipping. Wrap each loose end of wire around and around until all ends are wrapped tightly. You may need the help of needle-nose pliers to help bring the wire tight to the frame.

4. If you are making a heart, point the end of the wire and finish by shaping the top. Perfect the shape of your form until it is evenly shaped.

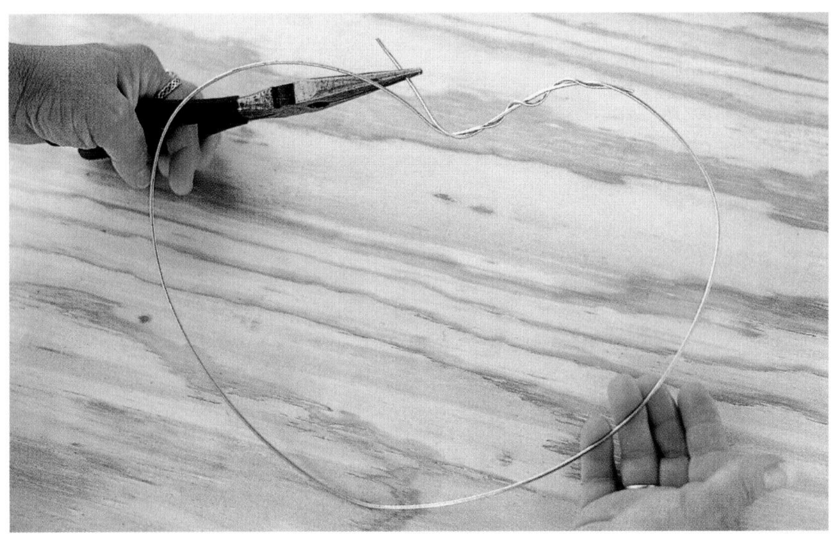

Making a wire foam base.

5. If you are using this form for a Spanish moss base, you are ready to proceed. If you are using this form for a handwired wreath, wrap the entire form with floral tape. The tape will help keep the material that is wired to the form from slipping on the wire.

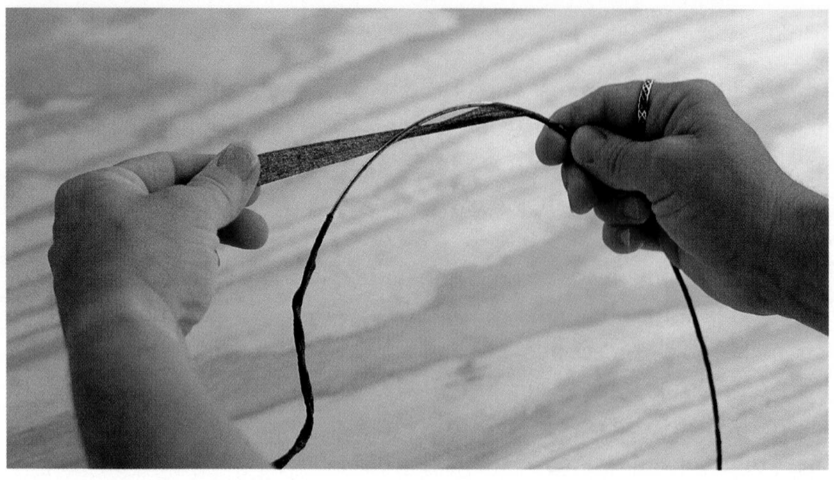

Wrapping the wire foam with floral tape.

Making a Spanish Moss Base

To make a Spanish moss base, you first need a wire form to work on. Once your wire form is made, follow the steps below to complete the Spanish moss base.

MATERIALS

- *florist wire*
- *wire-form base*
- *Spanish moss*
- *wire cutters*
- *scissors*

All Spanish moss is not created equal. Avoid buying Spanish moss if it looks coarse or dry. The finer moss is much easier to work with and will shed less.

1. Attach the loose end of a florist wire (22-gauge) to the wire form by wrapping the loose end around the form several times. Pull the wire taut to make sure it is securely attached.

2. Pull off a piece of Spanish moss. Pull the moss, forming it into a rope that is roughly the size you want for the thickness of the wreath base. When you have a nice length, wrap the moss around the wire form several times, then secure it by wrapping the florist wire around the moss.

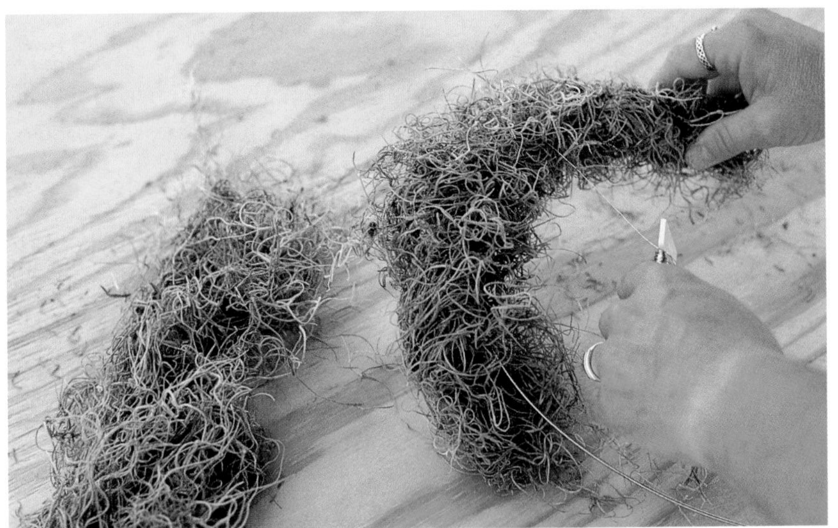

Making a Spanish moss base.

3. Continue to wrap the moss around the wire form, securing it with florist wire tightly. Keep making lengths of rope and securing it to the wire form until you have filled the entire wire form with moss.

4. Cut the florist wire, leaving about six inches attached to the form. Tuck the loose end of the wire in under a taut wire several inches away, and twist it around the taut wire until it is securely attached. Make a loop from this loose loop, and tighten it down by twisting it until it is tight. This will be your hanging loop. If the edges of the moss look shaggy, trim them with a pair of scissors.

A finished Spanish moss base and a partly wrapped cardboard base.

Making a Cardboard Base

As simple as it seems, a cardboard base is just what you need for some wreaths. Pine-cone wreaths, for example, are much more easily made on this type of form. The old method of wiring the cones around and around cannot measure up to using a simple cardboard base.

When making cardboard bases, keep the thickness of the cardboard in mind with the overall weight of the finished wreath. A pine-cone wreath will require a much heavier cardboard than a regular dried-flower wreath would.

Cardboard bases need to be wrapped with fabric in order to be both functional and attractive. Keep this in mind before you throw away those left-over fabric scraps.

MATERIALS

- *heavy cardboard*
- *dinner plate*
- *pencil*
- *box cutters*
- *heavy-duty scissors*
- *18-gauge wire*
- *thin strips of fabric*
- *glue gun and sticks*

1. Choose a clean, thick piece of cardboard from which you will make your base. Using a plate, or other form for a template, trace the outline for the base onto the cardboard. Trace the inner dimensions of the wreath as well. If the cardboard is not substantial enough, or if you need another thickness for an extra-heavy base, trace that outline now.

2. Use a box cutter or exacto blade to cut out the outside and inside dimensions of the wreath. Trim the edges, if necessary, with scissors.

3. Cut a piece of 18-gauge wire about eight inches long. Form a loop, then twist the wire together, leaving about three or four inches of wire at each end. Push these ends through the corrugation of the cardboard until they come out the other side, leaving the loop at the top of the form. This will be your hanging loop. Draw up the excess wire back toward the top of the form. Make sure that the wire stays in this position while the fabric is being wrapped around the form. By creating a loop in this fashion (rather than just gluing a loop on the form), you can be sure that the loop will stay in place, even on a heavy wreath.

4. Cut long, thin strips of fabric. For most wreath bases, fabric in strips one to two-and-a-half inches wide is easy to work with. Start at the wire hanger and glue the fabric down to the side of the form facing up with hot glue. Wrap the fabric around the cardboard form until it is all used up, then secure the end of the fabric with hot glue on the side of the base facing up.

You may have to cut the fabric in order to do this, but it will make a neater and more attractive form in the end. Glue down another piece of fabric where you left off, and continue wrapping fabric until the entire surface of the base has been covered.

Making a Handwired Wreath

The arranger who can make handwired wreaths is a versatile arranger. Your materials will go much farther, you can make your wreaths any shape and size you please, and nearly any filler can be made into a handwired wreath.

Suitable materials include fresh herbs, baby's breath, German statice, and dried herbs such as artemisia, Sweet Annie, and statice latifolia. Follow the instructions below for a surefire way to create a full, beautiful wreath every time! Beginners should try a round wreath first, and work their way toward the more difficult shapes.

MATERIALS

- *fillers such as baby's breath, statice, or Sweet Annie*
- *florist wire*
- *wire-form base*
- *wire cutters*

1. Gather the filler to be used for your wreath and trim the stems. Refer to the instructions for "Forming Flower Bundles" (page 77) before you start trimming, and keep in mind the size of the wreath you are working on when you decide on how long a stem to leave on the filler. Make a pile of trimmed material to work from; this makes your work flow much more quickly and easily.

2. Attach a paddle of florist wire to the wreath form, and leave it attached. This wire will be wrapped around the wire form each time you need to attach a bundle of filler to the form.

3. Once the stems have been trimmed, you can begin making and attaching the bundles to the form. Make the first bundle, then check it for size comparative to the overall planned size of the wreath. If the size of the bundle is right, even off the ends, leaving just about three to four inches of stem, not including the flower tops.

4. If you are right-handed, you will work in a clockwise manner; if you are left-handed, you will work counterclockwise. Once you place the first bundle on the wreath, you will be working around the form in one direction until you are finished. As you will see, it makes no difference where you start when you make a round wreath. Heart-shaped wreaths are worked by start-

Adding a second bundle to a handwired wreath.

ing at the dip in the heart, on the right if you are right-handed and on the left if you are left-handed. By working a heart-shaped wreath in this way, your hanging loop will be positioned properly when your wreath is finished.

5. Place the first bundle on the wire form. Be certain to keep the flowers on the "face" of the wreath—do not let the flowers slip to the outside or the inside surface of the form. To work comfortably, brace the wire form up against your body—this gives you a little more control of the form. When the flower bundle is in place, hold it onto the form with your thumb (your right thumb if you are left-handed, your left thumb if you are right-handed)—this leaves your other hand free to wrap the florist wire around the form. Wrap the wire very close to, but not on, the flowers. This will keep the flower bundle nice and full. You need only wrap the wire around two or three times to keep each bundle in place. If you make a habit of wrapping the wire more than this, and for any reason need to take a few bunches off, the extra wrapping makes a lot of work and frustration.

6. The placement of each succeeding bundle is important. If you place the bundle too far away from the last one, you will have a hole in the finished wreath. On the other hand, if you place the next bundle too close, you will use way too much material, and your work will look bunched up and cumbersome. Place each flower bundle so that it just covers the stems of the last one and so that there is no gap between bundles. Be sure to pull the wire taut between flower bundles so that the wire does not become loose on the back of the wreath. If you learn to work in this way, the flow of making these wreaths will come naturally to you in time.

Placing the last bundle on a handwired wreath.

7. Continue making and wiring bundles to the wire form, working around the form in the same direction you started. Check your work after every three or four bundles. Hang the wreath away from you so that you can get a good look at it from a distance. If you find any corrections that need to be made, go back and make them before you get too far along in your work.

8. Placement of the last bundle is critical. When the last flower bunch fills the final gap in the wreath, it is difficult to fit the bundle in place. To make this step easier, lift the flower tops from the first bundle and slide the stems from the last bundle under them. While still holding the flower tops, wire the last bundle to the form, leaving the wire to the back of the wreath when you are finished.

9. Cut off the florist wire, leaving a six-inch length. Loop the wire under another wire several inches away, then twist it down tightly. Make a small loop with this excess wire and twist it several times to make it secure. This will be your hanging loop.

If you are on a budget or do not have the time to grow your own filler, maybe fern wreath bases are for you. They can be made of bracken fern, which is plentiful in the wild, and free. The fern can be dyed before the base is made, or the entire wreath can be immersed in a dye bath. They are easy to make in a crimp-ring form.

Using Crimp-Ring Wreath Forms

Making a wreath on a crimp ring is very similar to making a handwired wreath. Instead of wiring each bundle on, bundles are placed in the form and the "fingers" are turned down over the flower stems to hold the bundles in place. These "fingers" are very flexible and fold down easily.

MATERIALS

- *crimp-ring form*
- *fillers such as baby's breath, statice*
- *wire*
- *wire cutters*

Making a crimp-ring wreath.

1. Place the form on a work surface with the open side facing you. The fingers of the form should be facing up.
2. Trim your filler material and make your first bundle, keeping in mind the overall size of the wreath. Leave the stems on the flower bundles roughly six inches in length—do not trim them as you would for a hand-wired wreath.
3. You will work this wreath in one direction around the form until the form has been filled. Keep the bundles loose and airy. At first, this may seem too sloppy or it may seem as though the flowers will come loose from the form. These forms just take a bit of getting used to, and dense, tightly packed bundles are just not suited to them.
4. Place the bundle in the form, then bend the fingers over the stems of the bundle, crossing them into an X. This will hold the bundle in place.
5. Make the next bundle and place it in the form. The stems of the last bundle should just be covered by the flower tops of the second flower bundle.

Cross over the fingers of the form to keep this bundle in place, and continue filling in the form until the base is completed.

6. If you reach a spot where there are no fingers to keep the material in place in the form, you can attach them to the form with a length of florist wire. This occasionally happens because the forms were originally intended for evergreen wreaths instead of the more delicate dried flowers. These wreaths are easily hung on a headed nail by the back of the form. No extra hanging loop is necessary.

7. If the crimp rings show once the wreath base has been completed, a little extra filler can be inserted to camouflage them.

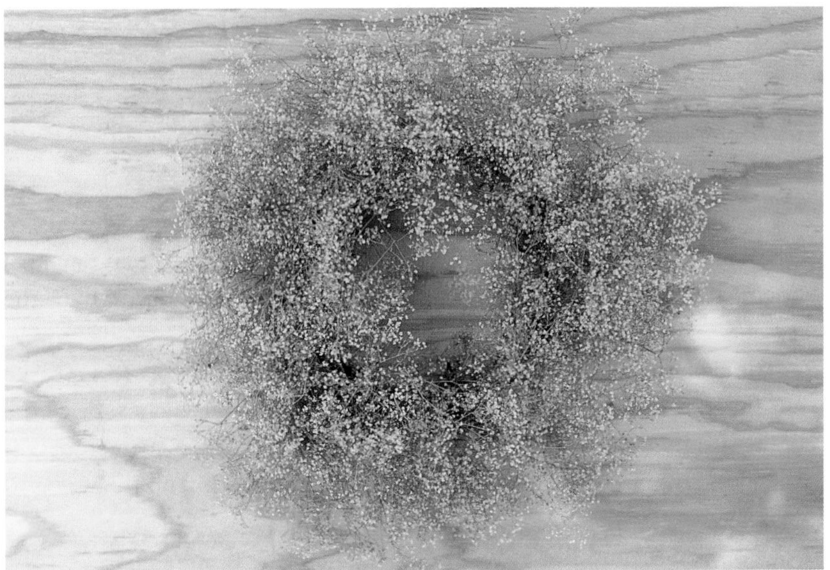

A finished crimp-ring wreath.

Making a Wreath on a Straw Form

Wreaths made on straw forms are large and impressive. They take a lot of material to complete. The filler material is pinned to the base with greening, or fern pins. First the inside edge of the wreath is completed, then the front of the wreath, and finally, the outside edge. As with other wreaths, these wreaths are worked around all in the same direction.

MATERIALS

- *straw wreath base*
- *fillers such as baby's breath, statice, Silver King artemisia*
- *18-gauge wire*
- *wire cutters*
- *greening pins*

Placing the second bundle on the inside edge of a straw base.

1. Place the wreath on your work surface. Cut an 18-gauge wire, six to eight inches long; insert it through the back of the wreath; and make a hanging loop with it. Turn the wreath base over. The top surface will be the face of the finished wreath.
2. Trim your filler material and make a large pile of it to work from. Make your first flower bundle, and trim the stems to about four inches. Place the bundle on the inner surface of the wreath form, then place a greening pin over the stems close to the flower heads, and push the pin all the way into the straw.
3. Make the second flower bundle. Place it so the flowers just cover the stems of the previous bundle, and secure it with a greening pin. Continue in this way until the entire inner surface of the wreath is covered.
4. Next work on the face of the wreath. Be certain to make the flower bundles large enough to cover the entire surface. Remember that these bundles will have to reach from those on the inside surface to those on the outside surface.
5. When the face of the wreath is complete, move to the outer edge. Keep working in the same direction as before. Place and pin bundles to the outer edge of the base until the wreath is complete.

COMPOSING A CENTERPIECE

Composing a centerpiece can be one of the most difficult tasks to learn in floral arranging. Although intimidating, all centerpieces really require is practice and a bit of patience.

MATERIALS

- *design bowl*
- *¼ block floral foam*
- *filler such as Silver King artemisia*
- *pruners or floral snips*

Below are some general guidelines that will get you started. Until you have perfected the method, practice by making centerpieces that measure about ten to twelve inches across.

1. Place the design bowl on your work surface. Cut about a quarter of the foam off a block of Sahara foam. Push the foam securely into the teeth in the bottom of the design bowl to secure the foam in place. Leave one long edge of the foam facing you as you work.

2. Trim your filler material, leaving stems about one foot long (these will be trimmed more). Shorter pieces are also useful, so set those aside in a separate pile. Make a good-sized pile of trimmed filler from which you can work.

3. There are few rules in floral arranging, but one of them refers directly to arrangement made on foam. Floral stems are never placed straight into the foam; they are always placed in the foam at an angle. The reason for this is simple: Nothing in nature is put together with straight lines. If your centerpiece is put together with straight angles, it will look totally unnatural. Keep this rule in mind as you work through making a centerpiece.

4. The first thing to establish when making a centerpiece is the overall size that the arrangement will be. For instructional purposes, our arrangement will be about twelve inches from side to side. Trim two pieces of filler to roughly a seven-inch length. Using the natural arch of the filler, place the stem in the foam on one of the short sides—the filler should arch down toward the tabletop. In this way the filler will eventually cover all visible signs of your design bowl. Place the other piece of filler in the opposite short side of the foam. Now you can see how wide your centerpiece will be.

5. Trim two stems of filler to lengths of about four inches, and trim four more stems to about three-inch lengths. Place the four-inch pieces in the center of each of the long edges of the foam, near the edge of the design bowl. Now you can fill the edge near the bowl with filler, and work up as you continue to fill. Be sure that the material arches downward. In the same manner, place the four shorter stems on each corner of the foam block. Stand directly over the design bowl and look down on it. You should be able to clearly see the outer parameters of your centerpiece. If any one piece looks out of alignment with the others, adjust it now.

Starting the outline of a centerpiece.

6. Next, trim a stem about ten to twelve inches long. Place this stem directly into the top of the foam block. You should now be able to see the overall size of the arrangement very well.

7. Begin to fill in the sides, front, and back of the centerpiece, trimming each stem just before it is placed in the foam. Place a stem or two on one side, then counter your actions by placing stems on the opposing side. Every

The centerpiece, partly filled in.

so often stand back and observe what you have done. By observing the piece in this way, you will be able to see the angle of the stems that will be needed to fill in a certain area.

8. When the sides are nearly filled, begin to work on the top of the foam. Remember that you do not want the centerpiece too high in the center, or folks on each side of your dinner table will not be able to converse. Again, by observing from a distance occasionally, you will be able to discern at what angle the stems need to be placed.

9. When the sides, front, back, and top are nearly finished, it is time to go back to each one and fill in any gaps that may show the foam underneath. Remember when you do this that short pieces fill in such gaps more quickly.

10. The base for your centerpiece is now finished and it is ready for you to add the accents and flowers of your choice.

CONSTRUCTING A SWAG

There are two ways to construct a swag. One method uses Sahara foam and the other method does not. The method used for a particular swag is dependent on the type of material used to create it.

For example, artemisia has long graceful stems and can be made into a swag easily without the use of foam. German statice, however, has short stems and needs the foam as a background on which you build the swag.

Below are instructions for creating swags using both methods.

Creating a Swag on Floral Foam

MATERIALS

- *sharp knife*
- *1 block of Sahara foam*
- *2 to 6 4-inch floral picks*
- *wire cutters*
- *18-gauge wire*
- *floral tape*
- *several bunches of German statice*

1. Slice the floral foam lengthwise into three pieces, about $1^1/_2$ inches wide. Each one of these pieces will form a small swag. To make a larger swag, use floral picks to join two of these pieces together along the short end. Make sure that they are joined securely.

The hanging loop for a swag, made with floral foam.

2. Slice off a triangular piece from each top corner of the foam with a sharp knife. This will give you a more natural swag shape to start with.

3. Cut a piece of wire about five inches long. Make a loop out of the wire, and attach the loop to a floral pick with floral tape. Place the pick into the center of the foam on the top and to the back of the foam. This will be your hanging loop.

4. Break the German statice into individual stems, and make a pile from which you can choose stems to work with. Always leave the stems long (they can always be cut down as you work, but you can never add length once it is gone). For a small swag, your stems should be anywhere from

The first step of making a swag on floral foam.

three to eight inches in length. It is helpful to make two or more piles, placing similar lengths in each pile.

5. Just as with other arrangements, you never place stems straight into the foam. Instead they are placed in the foam at slight angles that will give the finished piece a natural look. Always place the "face" of the flowers toward yourself as you work.

6. Begin the swag by placing a six-inch stem of statice on each side of the swag, just pushing the stems in a half inch or so. These first two pieces should help you establish the size of the swag from side to side. Place a four-inch stem in the **crown,** or top center of the swag. This stem should be roughly half the size of the first two. This will show you the ultimate height of the top of the swag.

7. Begin filling the foam with stems of statice, working first on the sides. Fill a bit on one side, then fill a bit on the opposite side. Working in this way you will not get too far ahead of yourself and any errors you may make are much easier to correct. Keep a close eye on the angles you are forming as you proceed. Keep the angles soft and natural-looking.

8. When the sides of the swag are nearly filled, begin working on the top. Generally the top of the swag calls for shorter pieces, angling away from the center. Fill first on one side, then move to the other side until the top has been filled.

9. Finish off the swag base by filling in any holes that remain. Be sure that no foam is visible between the stems of statice. Hold the swag up as if it were hanging on the wall. Make sure that no foam is visible from this viewpoint. If you can see foam between stems, fill these gaps with shorter stems

A finished swag on floral foam.

of statice less than three inches long—they will fill the gaps much more quickly than longer pieces.

Creating a Swag Base Without Floral Foam

MATERIALS

- *Sweet Annie, Silver King artemisia, or a similar filler material*
- *18-gauge wire*
- *wire cutters*
- *hot glue gun*

1. Remove the lower leaves from the Silver King stems and cut them to no longer than twenty-four inches in length. Trim up a pile from which you can work. You want to keep the flower tips and only those leaves that are silvery and clean. This may mean that some of the flowers will be very small or that some of the stems will be bare or short. Make piles of similar length material, as all these types of pieces will be used before you finish the swag base.

2. Select two full, large-flowered stems from your pile. Place them on your work surface, crossing the stems. Push the ends toward the center until the swag measures about twenty-four inches from tip to tip. This will be the finished size of the swag base. As you work, the swag base will lie on your work surface facing you. Always use the natural arch in your filler material to help form the swag. To create a nice graceful flow, the stems should arch down on each end of the swag.

3. Begin adding stems to each side of the swag base, trimming the stems and crisscrossing them as you work. Continue adding stems until each end

A swag—wired and ready to finish.

of the swag is full and graceful-looking. Hold up the swag by it center, making sure that you do not displace any of the stems. Check the swag base to be sure that the sides are similar in form and size. If they are not, add more stems until you are satisfied that they are even.

4. You will have about an eight-inch area of bare stem in the center of the swag base. This is normal and will be filled in later. Wrap the wire around the bare stems in the center of the swag and secure them by wrapping the wire around and around the stems until they are all wired tightly. Leaving about four inches on the end, cut the wire and tie off the two ends as tightly as you can to prevent any stems from loosening.

5. Now you are ready to fill in the bare stems toward the center of the swag base. The very center is where you will most likely want a bow, so this need not be filled in. Trim the shorter stems you set aside earlier; these will be glued into the base. Place a bead-sized glob of hot glue on the end of each stem, then gently slide the stem into place under a larger stem. The glue will catch hold on the existent stems, adding strength to the swag. Keep all the flowers flowing in the same direction as you fill. Very small flower ends can be used in the very center, just above and just below where your bow will be placed. Keep filling in this fashion until the base is filled except for the spot saved for a bow.

6. This type of swag is hung by impaling the stems on a headless nail until it hangs evenly.

MAKING A GARLAND

Garlands are very versatile, but are rarely used these days apart from the Christmas holidays. They are an excellent way to utilize greenery of almost any kind, but flowers can also be used.

Garlands can be hung under a window or picture, used around a door casing, or placed on a table or mantelpiece. Any way you use them they add classic elegance to your home.

MATERIALS

- *a length of twine or lightweight rope*
- *greenery of your choice—boxwood, running cedar, princess pine, dusty miller, or herb foliages*
- *C-clamp*
- *Paddle of 22-gauge florist wire*

1. Choose the rope or twine for your garland after you have chosen the foliage you will use. The twine should be light and flexible. If the twine is too stiff, the garland will not have a graceful look to it, but will look stiff and unnatural.

2. Cut the twine to the length that you want for the finished garland, adding about eight inches to this length. On each end of the twine, make a hanging loop. If your garland is very long, additional loops to help keep it in place can be added after it has been finished.

3. Using the C-clamp, attach one end of the twine to your work surface. This will help give tension to the garland as you work and will make it easier for you to place each bundle correctly without leaving gaps in the finished piece.

Wiring a garland.

4. Trim up the foliage for the garland, leaving short stems just as you would when making a handwired wreath. Make a pile of foliage from which to work.

5. Attach the florist wire to the end of the garland twine by twisting it around the twine several times. If you are right-handed, you will be more comfortable working from your left to right. If you are left-handed, vice versa.

6. Make a bundle of foliage and place it at the end of the garland twine. Hold it with one hand and loop the florist wire around the stems two or three times, just as if you were making a handwired wreath. Make the next bundle of foliage, and place it on the twine, just covering the stems of the previous bundle.

7. Continue making and placing bundles of foliage on the garland twine until you come to the end. Tie off the wire by cutting it off and twisting it around the twine several times so that it will not unravel.
8. If your garland is made of boxwood or princess pine it can be placed in a dye bath and dyed just as you would dye flowers. Deep green works well, and the color holds for a long time. Dying garlands is best done when the foliage is soft and fresh.

TOPIARY CONSTRUCTION

Topiaries are, in my opinion, the most poorly put together floral designs around. People just do not take the time to see that they are not top heavy or otherwise deficient. Topiaries are really not difficult to put together—they just take a few extra items and a bit of time. Follow these steps for perfect topiaries every time.

MATERIALS

- *wood trunk*
- *pot or other container for the base*
- *Styrofoam ball for the head*
- *hot glue gun*
- *moss to cover the foam and base*
- *greening pins*

1. When choosing the trunk for topiaries, choose attractive wood. Birch, fruit trees, or other trees with interesting bark work well. Collect trunks when you or neighbors trim trees or on walks through a local woodlot (but get permission first to trim). Choose only the wood that is straight-grained. Trim off all extra branches. Allow the trunks to dry for a minimum of three months in a warm, dry place. If the wood is still straight after it dries, it is fine to use for a topiary. In my opinion, cinnamon sticks are just too fragile to use for all but the smallest topiaries.
2. Pots used for topiaries should have some character. I have used small bowls that I have come across in a local china outlet, but I really think that a weathered clay pot works best. Check around under a potting bench for a pot that was unsuccessfully painted many years ago and has weathered nicely.
3. The head of the topiary should be made of Styrofoam (one of the best uses I have ever found for this obnoxious material). Using Styrofoam allows you to use German statice or other filler. It will also allow the trunk to be placed easily and securely. The trunk of the topiary should always be

attached before the head is finished. Choose a Styrofoam ball and mark a spot in the center where the trunk will be placed. Push the trunk into the foam about one inch and remove it. Using a high-temperature glue gun that has not heated up fully, place a big glob of glue in the hole made by the trunk. Put the trunk back in the hole and hold it straight and as still as you can while the glue sets up—this will take several minutes. Always use a high-temp glue gun that is not quite hot for this purpose—if the glue gun is up to full temperature, the glue will eat away the Styrofoam. I do not recommend low-temp glue guns for this purpose because they really do not hold heavy objects very well.

4. Place a loose covering of moss over the Styrofoam head of the topiary. Pin the moss to the Styrofoam with greening pins. Continue until the head is covered with moss, trimming off any excess.

5. You may position the topiary form in the pot before or after the head is finished. I think it is easier to work on the head before it goes into the pot. I place the trunk into a piece of Styrofoam I have set aside for this purpose—this frees up both of my hands when I am working.

6. When the topiary head is finished, it can be set in the pot. To accomplish this, I use a good quality patching plaster. Never use plaster of paris for this purpose. Mix the powder into a stiff paste with water. The thicker the paste, the faster it will set up in the pot. Plug the hole in the bottom of the pot with a piece of cardboard. Fill the pot to the rim. Place the topiary trunk in the pot as straight as you can, checking from all angles. Hold it firmly until the plaster has set, or brace it up against a wall for support.

EMBELLISHING ARTIFICIAL BASES

If you are too busy to create your own wreath base, or if you just like the look of an evergreen wreath, there is a way to make an artificial base look natural. I use such bases year-round, because I like the way they look. Here are a few tips to help make your plastic wreaths, garlands, or swags more realistic-looking.

1. Open out the branches of the wreath so that it is not flat; bring the branches out toward you at an angle. By opening up the wreath this way, you give yourself little pockets to fill with natural materials.

2. Spray the entire wreath with forest-green spray paint until all the brown or yellow tips of the plastic are covered. Be sure to give it a nice even coat.

3. Choose a filler material such as German statice or baby's breath. It may be sprayed or dyed a complementary color to the primary color you have chosen for the wreath, or you can use it as is. Make very small bundles and glue them into the foliage of the wreath in a random but steady pattern. You do not want to cover the entire wreath. Leave evergreen foliage visible between bunches of filler. This method will soften up the wreath base and pave the way for you to finish the wreath with a bow and the flowers of your choice for year-round enjoyment.

HOW TO FILL A BASKET

Baskets exist in many sizes and shapes, so there are few set rules when the time comes to fill them. One rule that must be followed is to place filler so that it follows the contour of the basket you have chosen. If the basket has a tall handle, the arrangement should match, having tall accents in the back of the arrangement. If the basket is low, with a low, wide handle, the arrangement should follow suit.

Starting the outline on a basket.

Many materials can be used for filler in baskets. German statice works very well, but I find baby's breath difficult to use. Artemisia and Sweet Annie work well, but other herb foliages tend to droop. A general flower basket made up of nothing but individual flower stems is also effective when it is done in varying shades of one color or mixed colors.

Sahara foam should always be used in the bottom of a basket arrangement if the flowers are to stay in place. The foam can be attached with double-sided tape, available at craft supply centers or where floral supplies are sold. This will prevent the foam from moving around in the basket—an annoying occurrence when you are concentrating on your work.

Remember the one rule of thumb when working with baskets: The stems never go straight into the foam. Everything is placed into the foam at an angle.

Part 3
The Designs

Hydrangea Wreath, Herb and Flower Wreath.

9 All-Season Designs

HYDRANGEA WREATH

MATERIALS

- *1 14-inch Spanish moss wreath base*
- *24–36 good-sized flower heads of Hydrangea paniculata*
- *1 yard pearl strand*
- *florist wire*
- *1 premade bow—mauve, pale green, or azalea pink—in the ribbon style of your choice*
- *hot glue gun*
- *floral picks*
- *24 heads of helichrysum, white or in shades of pink*
- *24 heads of pearly everlastings, natural or dyed mauve*
- *24 heads each of ammobium, natural and gomphrena, natural or dyed mauve*

Instructions:

1. Refer to the instructions for "Making a Spanish Moss Base" on page 82 to complete the base for this wreath. Put the hydrangea in a plastic shopping bag and dampen thoroughly with a mister. Close up the bag, shake it gently, and set it aside for about twenty minutes.

2. Make a figure eight from the pearl strand—each loop should be about three inches long. Keep looping the pearls back and forth until the entire strand is used. Cut a few inches of florist wire and wire around the center of the figure eight loops.
3. Choose a location for the bow at about four o'clock on the wreath base and glue it on securely. Glue the center of the pearl strand right on the top of or next to the bow. Hold securely in place with a floral pick until the glue has set. Spread the bow and the pearls out to make a full bow.
4. Check the hydrangea. It should be very soft—so soft that you can work with it without damaging it. Turn the flowers upside down and break off individual small stems of flowers—this will give you flowers that you can work with. Make a pile from which to work.
5. Take a small bunch in your fingers, then pinch and roll the stem between your fingers until a full bunch forms. There should be no ungainly gaps in the bunch of flowers. Place hot glue on the stem and glue it to the top of the base near the bow. As you work in this area, tuck a bit of each bunch under the bow to keep it erect, fluffy, and visible. If the flower stems are too small to use, place several together to make a bunch.
6. Continue adding bunches of hydrangea in this manner. As you work, choose five areas where you will place your accent flowers—these should be spaced sporadically and evenly around the wreath. Leave blank areas there to fill in later. Continue adding hydrangea bunches until the wreath is full except for these spots.
7. Place the helichrysum flowers in the spots left vacant. Next add the pearly everlastings and finally the smaller flowers to fill each of these areas.
8. Be sure to dry out any hydrangea you did not use so that it does not mildew. For the longest life, hang this wreath where it gets minimal light and does not get bumped often.

HERB AND FLOWER WREATH

MATERIALS

- *1 12-inch crimp-ring form*
- *3 to 6 extra-nice bunches of baby's breath, natural*
- *6 small bunches of sage*
- *1 large stem of Sweet Annie*
- *hot glue gun*
- *4 or 5 hydrangea flower heads*
- *12 to 15 field yarrow heads, dyed mauve*
- *24 santolina buttons, dyed mauve*

Instructions:

1. Refer to the directions for "Using Crimp-Ring Wreath Forms" on page 87 to complete the base for this wreath, using baby's breath in loose airy bunches to fill the form. If your bunches are too compact, they will not work well in this form.

2. Cut the stems of the sage to about three inches. Remove any inferior foliage that has yellowed or is not prime. Place stems individually into the baby's breath, placing two or three adjacent to form small compact bunches of foliage. Place them in the center and to the inside of the wreath. They should be spaced about two inches apart or so. You can place glue on the ends of the stems for added security if you like.

3. Break the Sweet Annie into stems about six inches long and tuck them into the baby's breath around the outer edge of the wreath. Do not be afraid to use two or three stems together if the Sweet Annie is fine—you want it to give the wreath a feathery edge and enough Sweet Annie to contrast with the background.

4. Spray the hydrangea with water to soften. Trim the flower stems and make six or eight small, full bunches. These should be placed and glued evenly around the center of the wreath. Make sure that each bunch is full by pinching and rolling the stems between your fingers until the hydrangea is nice and full.

5. Place and glue the dyed field yarrow between bunches of hydrangea, filling in the gaps. Place the dyed santolina buttons filling in between the field yarrow flowers.

SILVER KING ARTEMISIA WREATH

MATERIALS

- *1 12-inch crimp-ring form*
- *1 premade raffia bow, natural or dyed navy, royal, or country blue*
- *hot glue gun*
- *4 to 6 dozen stems Silver King artemisia*
- *1 large stem of Sweet Annie*
- *1 or 2 bunches of foxtail millet or other ornamental grass*
- *1 bunch of yarrow, dyed navy, royal, or country blue*
- *2 bunches of baby's breath, sprayed country blue*

- *12 heads of pearly everlasting, dyed navy, royal, or country blue*
- *24 santolina buttons, dyed navy, royal, or country blue*
- *1 stem of annual statice, dyed navy, royal, or country blue*
- *2 bunches of nigella pods*

Instructions:

1. Refer to the instructions for "Using Crimp-Ring Wreath Forms" on page 87 to complete the Silver King artemisia base for this wreath.

2. Choose a spot for the bow and glue it in place. Break the Sweet Annie into eight- to ten-inch stems. Place it in the wreath base, creating a wispy look around the outer edge. Add enough so that there is good contrast between it and the artemisia. Break the stems of the ornamental grass into similar lengths and place them in the wreath in the same fashion around the outer edge. You may use a small amount of hot glue on the ends of the stems for extra strength if you wish.

4. Cut the stems of the yarrow to about four inches in length. Glue the yarrow around the wreath in the center, leaving an even amount of space between flowers. Six or seven yarrow heads should fill the wreath nicely.

5. Make small, delicate bunches of baby's breath and glue them sporadically throughout the wreath base to the inside and outside edges.

6. Place and glue the pearly everlastings to fill the spaces between the yarrow flowers. Next, add the santolina buttons and annual statice to fill in the remaining gaps. Space them evenly and leave enough of the artemisia showing to give contrast to the piece.

7. Add the nigella pods as final accents around the inner and outer edge of the wreath.

When placing flowers in any arrangement, keep in mind this working order: First place any tall, long, or accent flowers; then choose the largest flowers and place them; fill spaces between them with medium-sized and smaller flowers. This will help you space the flowers well and will give the finished piece a more orderly appearance.

ARTEMISIA SWAG

Artemisia makes a fine base, but needs contrasting foliage to look its best. Choosing one primary color for the dyed flowers in this piece creates a clean look.

MATERIALS

- *artemisia base for swag*
- *2 large stems of Sweet Annie*
- *hot glue gun*
- *2 bunches of foxtail millet or other grass*
- *2 bunches of nigella pods*
- *3 teasels, dyed navy, royal, or country blue*
- *48 or more stems of Silver King artemisia*
- *1 bunch of yarrow, dyed navy, royal, or country blue*
- *2 bunches of achillea the pearl*
- *gomphrena, santolina buttons, or thistle heads, dyed navy, royal, or country blue*
- *florist wire*

Instructions:

1. Refer to the instructions for "Creating a Swag Base Without Floral Foam" on page 96 to complete the artemisia base for this swag.

emisia Wreath, Swag, and Centerpiece.

2. Break the Sweet Annie down into stems of about one foot long. Beginning at the inside of each side of the swag, begin tucking Sweet Annie into the swag—you can use a little glue on the ends of the stems for extra security. Use enough Sweet Annie so that the contrast between it and the artemisia shows up well. Put the Sweet Annie throughout the swag on both sides.

3. Place the foxtail millet as you did the Sweet Annie on both sides of the swag. Place the seed heads near the ends of the swag to good effect. The ends of the stems may be glued for extra holding power.

4. Break the stems of the nigella pods into lengths about four inches long. Place nigella throughout the swag as you did with the millet and Sweet Annie. The ends of the stems may be glued for extra holding power.

5. Cut the stems on the teasels to about two inches long. Glue them securely in the center of the swag where a bow would normally go. If they do not completely cover the stems in the center, you can fill with short pieces of Silver King flowers.

6. Cut the stems on the yarrow to about six inches long. Glue them in place on the swag, keeping the larger flowers closer to the center and the smaller flowers farther from the center. You may break some of the flowers into smaller pieces if they are too large and out of proportion.

7. Break the stems of the achillea the pearl into four-inch lengths. Place small groupings throughout the swag, gluing them in as you work. In each spot where there is a small bunch of achillea, glue one or two gomphrena flowers or santolina buttons for contrast.

ARTEMISIA CENTERPIECE

MATERIALS

- *1/3 block Sahara foam*
- *3 to 4 dozen stems Silver King artemisia*
- *1 stem of Sweet Annie*
- *1 bunch of yarrow, dyed navy blue*
- *1 bunch of baby's breath, sprayed with country blue paint*
- *6-inch floral picks*
- *floral tape*
- *12 santolina buttons, dyed navy, royal, or country blue*
- *12 heads of pearly everlasting, dyed navy, royal, or country blue*
- *glue*
- *1 floral design bowl*

Instructions:

1. Refer to the instructions "Composing a Centerpiece" on page 90 to prepare the base for this centerpiece with the artemisia.
2. Cut stems of Sweet Annie to about ten-inch lengths and insert them in the foam, spacing them well throughout the centerpiece.
3. Cut the yarrow stems to about ten inches in length. Place the stems of the yarrow into the foam, spreading the flowers evenly throughout. The larger flowers should go in the most visible locations, and the smaller flowers can be used to fill in.
4. Make small bunches of baby's breath and attach them to floral picks—six or seven bunches should be enough. Use floral tape to secure the stems to the pick. Place the picked baby's breath in the foam, again filling in the gaps between the yarrow flowers.
5. Using the santolina and pearly everlasting, fill in any remaining obvious gaps in the centerpiece. The santolina can be placed in the foam on the stem. The pearly everlastings may be picked and placed in the foam or they may be glued in place.

STATICE AND ROSEBUD HEART WREATH

MATERIALS

- *1 12-inch heart-shaped Spanish moss wreath base*
- *1 premade hunter-green bow in the ribbon style of your choice*
- *4 dozen miniature rosebuds*
- *hot glue gun*
- *2 bunches of German statice, stems cut into 2- to 4-inch lengths*
- *several stems of boxwood dyed hunter green and cut into 2-inch stems*

Instructions:

1. Refer to the instructions for "Making a Spanish Moss Base" on page 82 to complete the base for this wreath. Glue the bow to the center dip in the heart. Let the glue set, then spread the bow.
2. Beginning on one side of the bow, glue stems of statice to the wreath, just tucking the end of the stem into the moss base enough so that the glue catches and will hold the stem in place. It is more effective to put the glue

Statice and Rosebud Heart Wreath.

on each stem individually so that there is a minimum of glue showing through when you are done. All the stems of statice should point in the same direction and go with the flow of the shape of the wreath. Each stem of statice should stand up off the surface of the moss an inch or so.

3. Be sure to cover the width of the base from side to side so that no bare moss shows on either side of the stems of statice. Work by placing several stems across in a row and then moving on to the next area—this way you will cover the base more thoroughly. Keep gluing stems to the base until you come to the point of the heart.

4. Return to the top of the wreath and complete the other side of the wreath base starting at the top and working to the point at the bottom of the heart. Look over the base, filling in any gaps that you find.

5. Using a small dab of glue on the end of the stem, begin placing rosebuds on the wreath. They should be placed randomly but evenly around the base, perhaps leaving an inch between buds. Continue placing them until the wreath has been studded with them.

6. Glue the boxwood into the wreath in the same way that the rosebuds were applied. Use the foliage to hide any spot where glue may show through and be visible. Start on one side of the wreath and work to the

Victorian Flower Wreaths.

other side until the effect of the boxwood is accomplished and glue is camouflaged.

VICTORIAN FLOWER WREATHS

This versatile wreath can be made from any number of flowers as long as they are proportionate to the size of the wreath. Some field yarrow lends the piece an overall old-fashioned feel. The wreath is worked on the face of a moss base, leaving the inside and outside edges unadorned.

Small Victorian flower wreaths serve well as candle rings for any dinner table.

MATERIALS

- *1 Spanish moss base in the size and shape of your choice*
- *hot glue gun*
- *streamers to match bow*
- *1 premade satin ribbon bow*
- *12 to 15 helichrysum heads in shades of the color of your choice*
- *1 bunch of annual statice in an accenting shade*
- *several heads each of gomphrena and ammobium, natural or dyed in the color of your choice*
- *18 heads of pearly everlasting, natural*
- *24 heads of field yarrow, natural*
- *several stems of boxwood, dyed hunter green*
- *1 small bunch of statice latifolia*

Instructions:

1. Refer to the instructions for "Making a Spanish Moss Base" on page 82 to complete the base for this wreath. Glue the streamers in the center of the wreath at the top of the form, fanning them out to the sides. Glue the bow on top of the streamers, hiding where the streamers come together.

2. Place the helichrysum heads around the wreath in the center of the moss base—keep them spaced so that there is room between them for the smaller flowers. When you are satisfied with the arrangement, glue them in place.

3. Finishing this wreath is a matter of filling the remaining space on the face of the base. Start on one side and work systematically toward the other. Flowers in shades of the primary color you have chosen will be set to their best advantage if you situate them with white or ivory flowers nestled between them for contrast. Ammobium, pearly everlasting, statice, or field yarrow all work well.

4. Continue working around the wreath, alternating placing, and gluing colored and neutral flowers in this way until the entire wreath's surface is covered.

5. Break the boxwood stems into small pieces about two inches long. Glue these in place, spacing them evenly around the wreath, to contrast with the flowers.

6. Break the statice latifolia in small pieces about two inches in length. Glue them onto the wreath just as you did the boxwood to give a delicate look to the finished wreath.

GORGEOUS GERMAN STATICE WREATH

MATERIALS

- *1 12-inch wire-form wreath base*
- *1 hand-wired wreath*
- *12 deep rose or burgundy helichrysum heads*
- *hot glue gun*
- *12 heads of pearly everlastings, dyed burgundy*
- *15 to 18 nigella pods*
- *1 small bunch of Sweet Annie or ornamental grass, dyed burgundy*
- *4 to 6 bunches of top-grade German statice*
- *24 gomphrena flowers, dyed burgundy*

Instructions:

1. Refer to the instructions for "Making a Handwired Wreath" on page 85 to complete the base for this wreath.

2. Place the helichrysum heads around the wreath, spacing them evenly and keeping them to the center of the wreath. When you are satisfied with the arrangement, glue them in place.

3. Place the pearly everlasting flowers next, working them in between the helichrysum flowers. Next place the nigella pods toward the outer edge of the wreath.

4. Place the Sweet Annie or ornamental grass along the outside edge of the wreath, creating a wispy edge. Use the German statice and gomphrena flowers to fill in between the larger flowers.

GERMAN STATICE TOPIARY

MATERIALS

- *1 completed topiary base*
- *2 or more bunches of German statice*
- *1 Styrofoam ball of proportionate size*
- *1 clay pot*
- *18 heads of helichrysum, deep rose or burgundy*
- *1 bunch of astilbe, sprayed burgundy*
- *36 gomphrena flowers, dyed burgundy*
- *24 heads of pearly everlastings, dyed burgundy*
- *36 salal leaves*

Instructions:

1. Refer to the instructions for "Topiary Construction" on page 99 to complete the base for this topiary. I prefer to do everything but secure the

Gorgeous German Statice Wreath and Topiary, Victorian Flower Topiary.

topiary in the pot before I begin working on the head itself, because the pot becomes very heavy and cumbersome when you are working.

2. Cut the statice down into lengths that are proportionate to the size head you will be constructing. For a topiary head six or seven inches across, stems about three inches long do well. If your topiary head is larger or smaller, size them accordingly. No two lengths of statice will or should be the same. You need some variation in length, or the topiary will look trimmed and unnatural.

3. Begin by placing a stem of statice in each side of the Styrofoam halfway up the side of the head to establish the width. Place a piece in the top to establish the height, then a few shorter pieces around the base to establish the bottom edge. Check these from afar to see that they look in proportion, making adjustments if necessary.

4. Begin to fill from the pieces on the bottom to one on the side of the head, sizing the statice pieces so that the contours you create look natural. Stop and examine your work often, making corrections where necessary. Once you have a line filled from the bottom to the side, fill in that quarter of the Styrofoam fac-

A topiary head in the stand.

A German statice topiary in progress.

ing you. Next, go to the other side of the head, working until the bottom half of the head is filled.

5. Complete the half of the topiary head that is facing you by filling the top quarters in the same way you did the bottom quarters. Turn the head around and complete the other half in the same fashion. Check for and fill any gaps that allow Styrofoam to show through the statice base.

TIP: When placing filler in Styrofoam, it is not necessary to use hot glue. The pieces should not be placed straight into the foam. Place them in at an angle using the flow of the material to its best advantage and making sure that the face of the flowers face the viewer of the piece. Once you have had some practice, you will not even have to think about placing pieces in at an angle—it will come naturally to you, and your hands will remember what to do.

6. Prepare and set the topiary in the pot of your choice, referring to the instructions on page 100.

7. Glue the helichrysum flowers to the topiary head, evenly spacing them throughout the piece. Next, place the astilbe spikes, keeping them just slightly longer than the German statice itself. Fill the head with the gomphrena, pearly everlasting, or other accent flowers you have chosen, taking care to space them evenly. Leave enough of the German statice showing through the topiary to enjoy it and create contrast.

8. Finish the piece by evenly spacing salal leaves in the statice, allowing them to protrude slightly.

TIP: When working on topiaries, it is often advantageous to have two hands free to work with. To accomplish this, I bought a round chunk of Styrofoam in which the trunk can be inserted—the topiary stands erect as I work, and my work goes more quickly and easily.

When creating your own design, you do not have to use flowers that match in color perfectly. Instead, use flower colors in the same shade of one primary color. By doing so, you will give your arrangement a depth and appeal that would otherwise be lost.

VICTORIAN FLOWER TOPIARY

This topiary is constructed in the same way as the German Statice Topiary, except for the topiary head. Spanish moss is used to cover the Styrofoam, and the head is covered with wall-to-wall flowers. Any standard dried flower can be used, as long as it is not too large or does not stand too high up off the Styrofoam ball.

MATERIALS

- *1 completed topiary base*
- *greening pins*
- *Spanish moss*
- *1 Styrofoam ball of proportionate size*
- *sharp scissors*
- *glue*
- *24 to 30 helichrysum flowers in white and shades of pink*
- *patching plaster*
- *1 small bunch of statice latifolia*
- *sheet moss*
- *24 heads each of the following flowers in shades of white, ivory, and pink: pearly everlastings, gomphrena, ammobium, field yarrow, achillea the pearl, annual statice*

Note: santolina buttons, gomphrena, and yarrow can be dyed and used in this piece.

Instructions:

1. Refer to the instructions for "Topiary Construction" on page 99 to complete the base for this topiary. Construct the topiary up to the point of setting it in the patching plaster. Using greening pins, secure a good layer of Spanish moss all over the Styrofoam ball thick enough so that the Styrofoam cannot be seen. Trim the moss with sharp scissors to remove any excess.

2. Begin the topiary by gluing the helichrysum flowers on the head—spread them evenly around the head, as they will be the main flower in it. When gluing flowers on this type of topiary, you want them to stay as low to the Styrofoam ball as possible so that the topiary retains a round shape. This is especially true when placing flowers on the bottom.

3. Now that the main flowers are in place, you should work from the bottom up. Turn the topiary head upside down to work.

TIP: As with the Victorian Flower Wreath, it is important to keep the more brightly colored flowers separated from each other by placing white or ivory flowers in between them. If you use a good deal of field yarrow to accomplish this, it will give the topiary a charming, old-fashioned look.

Fill in between the helichrysum flowers with the assortment of accent flowers you have chosen for this topiary. Fill in a small section of the bottom, then move on to the next. Continue in this way until the bottom third of the topiary head is complete.

4. Turn the topiary right side up. Continue to fill the spaces between helichrysum flowers completely, finishing off one section at a time. Hold the topiary head away from you and check it often to be sure it has retained a nice round shape. Continue in this fashion until the entire head is covered with flowers.

5. Break the statice latifolia down into three-inch stems. Using a little glue, insert some of the filler sporadically around the topiary head. Keep the lengths even and the flow of the pieces in tune with the contour of the topiary.

6. Refer back to page 100 for instructions on setting the topiary in patching plaster. Finish the base with sheet moss. You may add a bow at the bottom of the trunk if you desire.

SEASHELL WREATHS

Each seashell wreath is unique. They can be made round or oval, in any size you like, but a twelve-inch wreath is surprisingly heavy. If you make a big one, be sure to hang it on a nail that is anchored in a stud.

Seashell wreaths also work well if done all in one shell.

MATERIALS

- *1 12-inch heavy cardboard base, wrapped with sturdy fabric—make sure that the base has an especially strong hanging loop*
- *a wide assortment of sea shells, medium and small in size*
- *any other seaworthy items you may have, such as crab claws, sea sponge, cork, small driftwood pieces, starfish, or coral*
- *hot glue gun*
- *Spanish moss*
- *decorative cord in any complementary shade*

Instructions:

1. Refer to the instructions for "Making a Cardboard Base" on page 84 to complete the base for this wreath. Sort the shells into two piles: larger and smaller. Set aside any that are special, unique in form, or otherwise unusual. Set aside crab claws and other items that can be used to emphasize the sea shore effect—these will be glued on last.

2. Using a hot glue gun, glue a thin layer of Spanish moss to the base; be especially sure that it comes to the outer edge of the wreath.

3. For the first layer, glue the larger shells to the wreath base; because of their weight, don't spare the glue. Make sure that you bring some shells over the inner and outer edge of the base. The edge of these wreaths should be a little irregular, and you do not want to see the cardboard base underneath. Continue gluing until a base layer of shells has been formed.

4. Glue the smaller shells over the top, positioning them on top of the first layer of shells. Make sure that all of the base is being covered. This will take quite a bit of time to get the depth and coverage you want. Last, sporadically glue on any special shells or other unusual pieces that you have saved aside.

5. Wrap the cord around the base and secure it on the back of the form.

WHIMSICAL BARK CURL

Seashell Wreath, Whimsical Bark Curl.

This type of bark curl is fairly common in woodlots and in the forest (but never strip bark off a tree—it is usually fatal to the tree). Such a piece makes a quick and easy gift or accent for your home.

MATERIALS

- *drill*
- *bark "curl" such as the one pictured*
- *hot glue gun*
- *piece of plywood or heavy cardboard about 10 inches long by 4 inches wide*
- *2 screw eyes and 22-gauge wire; 6 inches of wire for hanging loop (for cardboard backing only)*
- *enough felt to cover the plywood*
- *sheet moss*
- *a bird's nest, real or purchased*
- *piece of honeycomb*
- *a few small pine cones, lichens, or other woodsy items*
- *feather bird (a nuthatch or woodpecker is most believable)*
- *raffia bow*

Instructions:

1. Attach the bark and create a background and hanger for the piece as described in steps 1 and 2 of the Birch Bark Swag (pages 123–124). If you use cardboard for a background, form a hanging loop with the 6-inch piece of wire. Glue the loop to the top edge of the cardboard securely. Cover the cardboard with felt, as described in steps 1 and 2 of the Birch Bark Swag (see pages 123–124).

2. Cut and glue sheet moss to the front of the background—fitting it around the bark curl and leaving it jagged and natural-looking.

3. Place the bird's nest in the bark curl or glue it directly to the surface of the bark.

4. Glue the honeycomb and other woodsy items to the bark curl, spacing them out—you want the piece to look as though you just picked it up off the forest floor.

5. Glue the feather bird to the bark in a whimsical position, and affix the raffia bow to one side with a dab of hot glue.

BIRCH BARK SWAG

This wonderful swag is a one-of-a-kind piece. If you are lucky enough to find a nice piece of birch bark, you can make one, too. The directions following are for this particular piece of bark; you may find you will need to make some adjustments for the wood you find.

MATERIALS

- *cordless drill with $^1/_8$-inch drill bit*
- *1 unique bark "curl"*
- *hot glue gun*
- *2 small screws*
- *1 piece of $^1/_4$-inch plywood, about 12 inches long by 4 inches wide*
- *a piece of felt large enough to cover the back of the plywood*
- *2 screw eyes*
- *22-gauge wire*
- *1 block Sahara foam*
- *several large stems of Sweet Annie*
- *8 to 12 poppy heads, gilded gold or sprayed with red spray paint*
- *8 to 12 pheasant feathers, hawk feathers, or turkey feathers*
- *8 to 12 sensitive fern or ostrich fern fronds, gilded gold*
- *2 bunches of foxtail millet or other decorative grass*
- *1 premade plaid bow of your choice (optional)*

Instructions:

1. Drill two holes about ten inches apart in the back side of the bark curl (the open end faces up). Use two small screws to securely attach the curl to the piece of plywood. If the screws go through the plywood, cover them with hot glue so that they will not scratch the wall surface.

2. Cover the back of the plywood with felt, gluing it to the surface and folding it over the edges of the plywood cleanly and neatly so that the entire back is covered. Attach the screw eyes securely to the top of the plywood, one on each end. String the wire through the screw eyes to form the wire hanger for this piece.

3. Place the block of Sahara foam in the bark cavity. If an entire block does not fit, cut it down to size it accordingly.

4. Cut the stems of Sweet Annie down to a size that is proportionate with the length of the bark curl you have. Place the Sweet Annie into the foam—first one side and then the other—to set the outer parameters of the piece. Now place a piece that will set the limit for the top of the arch. Keep the stems at an angle to the foam and do not make them overly long—from the bark to the top of the piece is about twelve to fifteen inches for the swag pictured.

5. Fill in the swag using the Sweet Annie—you will have to use long pieces and some shorter pieces, too, to achieve the look you want and to cover the foam in front. Continue filling until finished.

Birch Bark Swag.

6. Cut the poppy stems to the correct length and place them in the foam, fanning them out and spacing them evenly through the piece. Next, add the feathers in the same fashion. Then add the fern fronds, spacing them around and filling in between the poppy heads and feathers. Last, place the foxtail millet as an accent throughout the swag, using its graceful seed heads to add to the flow of the swag.

7. I chose a plaid bow for this piece. A metallic bow would also look lovely. Glue the bow onto the bark. This piece can have a very long life; if your filler begins to fade, simply replace it. You may wish to spray the bark with a clear lacquer spray to bring out the natural grain of the wood.

Fall Designs

CHINESE LANTERN WREATH

Chinese Lantern Wreath, Fall Harvest Wreath.

This wreath makes a simple, yet undeniable statement that fall has arrived.

MATERIALS

- *1 14-inch crimp-ring form*
- *2 or 3 large bunches of statice latifolia*
- *copper spray paint*
- *hot glue gun*
- *6 to 8 stems of Chinese lanterns*
- *24 salal leaves*
- *1 small bunch of* nigella *Transformer*

Instructions:

1. Refer to the instructions for "Using Crimp-Ring Wreath Forms" on page 87 to complete the base of this wreath using statice latifolia.
2. Lightly spray the wreath base with the copper spray paint, until a nice copper color develops.
3. Cut the Chinese lantern stems down to single groupings of lanterns. Glue them to the wreath in spokes that radiate to the outside of the wreath, as in the wreath shown. Each spoke should have several lanterns in it and the spokes should not be too far apart.
4. Place and glue in the salal leaves, working them to the inner and outer part of the wreath for an accent. Cut the nigella stems down to three inches and glue one nigella head on the inside of each Chinese lantern spoke.

FALL HARVEST WREATH

This wreath is truly beautiful. Although the statice does fade in time, the colors in this piece fade subtly together and look great for many years.

MATERIALS

- *1 10-inch wire form*
- *3 or 4 bunches of German statice*
- *12 salmon helichrysum flowers*
- *hot glue gun*
- *several bunches of pepperberries*
- *3 heads of wild quinine*
- *1 small bunch each of salmon and pale yellow annual statice*
- *12 to 15 pieces of lunaria*
- *24 santolina buttons, natural*
- *18 heads of ammobium*
- *several stems boxwood, natural*

Instructions:

1. Refer to the instructions for " Making a Handwired Wreath" on page 85 to make the base for this wreath using German statice.

2. Begin placing the helichrysum on the wreath, spacing them out evenly and keeping them to the center of the wreath. Glue them on securely. Next add the pepperberries, keeping them to the outside. Since they are the brightest item on this wreath, make sure that you use good-sized bunches.

Corn husk can be dyed and stapled into a loop to add a colorful touch to most any wreath. Dye them in bright, jewel-tone colors and add them to fall or southwestern designs.

3. Break down the heads of wild quinine and begin to fill in between the larger flowers with it.

4. Next, place the salmon and pale yellow statice throughout the wreath, working it to the inside and outside edges and filling any gaps with it. Glue it on securely.

5. Place and glue the lunaria pods along the outer edge of the wreath so that they are highly visible. Then add the santolina buttons and ammobium gluing them in and working them to the inner and outer edges of the wreath. Finally, add short stems of boxwood along the outer and inner edges of the wreath as an accent.

CORKSCREW WILLOW SWAG

MATERIALS

- *a good pile of small- to medium-sized corkscrew willow branches and twigs—green and pliable*
- *1 crimp-ring form for a swag*
- *one premade plaid or striped bow, or another bow of your choice*
- *hot glue gun*
- *24 salal leaves*
- *several small bunches of pepperberries*
- *small bunch of statice latifolia*

Instructions:

1. Cut down the corkscrew willow twigs to usable sizes. Make a pile of medium-sized twigs and small twigs.

2. Refer to the instructions for "Using Crimp-Ring Wreath Forms" on page 87. A swag is made in the same way, but you will work from one end to the other.

3. Place the larger twigs in the crimp form on one end, facing the small end of the twigs in one direction. Work in some of the smaller twigs over

Corkscrew Willow Swag.

the larger ones to add detail. You want as many twisted twigs as possible to be evident in the piece.

4. Crimp the ring over the twigs to hold them in place and then put another bunch of twigs into the frame. Place smaller twigs over the large ones, crimp the ring, and continue to work until the swag is two-thirds completed. Now start at the other end and reverse the direction of the twigs as they go into the frame.

5. When you can no longer put twigs into the frame, there will be a gap left—this is where the bow is placed. Glue the bow on securely.

6. There will be rings showing in front of the twigs; to cover them up, glue the salal leaves all along the front of the swag where the rings come together. On top of the leaves, glue several large bunches of pepperberries. This should totally camouflage the crimp rings.

7. Finally, cut down some of the statice latifolia and glue it into place all throughout the swag. You may want to spray the swag with a clear spray lacquer.

BIRDFEEDER WREATH

This unusual wreath will keep the birds coming to your yard to feed until it is devoured. It makes a great gift for your favorite bird lover.

Birdfeeder Wreath, Grass Wreaths.

MATERIALS

- *1 12-inch vine wreath base*
- *12-gauge wire*
- *1 or 2 small sunflower heads with the seed formed*
- *1 or 2 packages of canary millet on the stem (available at pet shops)*
- *hot glue gun*
- *wild centurea seed heads and purple coneflower seed heads*
- *assorted wild grasses such as foxtail millet, wheat, barley, squirrel's tail grass*

Instructions:

1. Make a hanger for the wreath using the 12-gauge wire.

2. Cut the stem of the sunflowers to about three inches, and wire through the stems. Wire the sunflower heads directly to the vine base.

3. Cover the remainder of the base with canary millet—it may be wired onto the base or tied on with nylon fishing line. Gluing it on is less sturdy and may not hold up to the elements. Over the top of the millet, glue on any wild centurea heads or purple coneflower heads you may have, filling in any gaps left in the millet.

4. Use a glue gun to attach the wild grasses—they should be glued under the sunflowers and millet onto the back to give the wreath a more aesthetic look. Continue gluing until grasses create the entire outer edge of the wreath.

GRASS WREATHS

Effective wreaths can be made from the simplest materials—in this case grasses or Sweet Annie. I have used foxtail millet, hare's tail grass, wheat, and Sweet Annie in the past. The simplicity of the material adds to their beauty.

MATERIALS

- *wire-form wreath (I have used 3 to 8 inches for the wreaths in the photo on page 129)*
- *several bunches of the grass of your choice*
- *florist wire*

Instructions:

1. Use the instructions for "Making a Wire-Form Base" and "Making a Handwired Wreath" on pages 80 and 85, respectively. You may make any size form you wish; these wreaths are quite effective in large or small sizes. Larger sizes take a huge volume of material to complete.
2. When working up these wreaths in grasses, keep in mind the stiffness or relaxed nature of the stems you are working with. Those with less rigid stems need to be wired quite close to the seed heads to keep them from looking droopy.

FALL WALL BASKETS

These flat wall baskets, designed for a hanging display, are easy to fill even for the beginner. The one pictured on page 132 makes a nice simple accent on a door or wall.

MATERIALS

- *small pieces of Sahara foam to fit the basket*
- *small wall baskets (narrow pockets are best)*
- *small stems of any grasses such as hare's tail or foxtail millet*
- *small stems of Sweet Annie*
- *1 small bunch of German statice*
- *small assortment of small flowers—yarrow, ammobium, nigella pods, immortelle, bee balm, santolina, lavender flowers, and salvia flowers are all good*

Instructions:

1. Place the foam snugly into the pocket of the wall basket. Trim off any excess so that no foam is showing.
2. Trim the stems of the statice, Sweet Annie, and grasses. Determine the length you will need by holding the flowers against the outline of the basket's handle—the handle is the outline for the flowers. Don't forget to allow for some of the stem that will be placed in the foam.
3. Begin placing the statice in the foam. First form the back of the arrangement. Once this is done, trim some shorter stems and use them to form the front of the arrangement; these stems will face directly out toward the viewer. Continue until an outline for the arrangement has been formed.
4. Begin to place the grass and Sweet Annie as accents—you will not need much if your baskets are small. Place these accenting foliages in a fan-like shape.
5. Finish the baskets by placing the flowers in the foam—the larger flowers should be placed first, then the smaller flowers are used to fill. Flowers such as ammobium can be glued directly to the fillers.

WOODLAND BARK AND MOSS WREATH

This subtle beauty will remind you of a walk in the woods each time you look at it.

MATERIALS

- *1 12-inch oval Spanish moss base*
- *1 large piece of sheet moss*
- *hot glue gun*
- *4 to 5 medium-sized bark curls*
- *18 larch cones*
- *2 or 3 pieces of reindeer moss, treated*
- *small feathers or other interesting woodland items*
- *honeycomb*
- *several smaller pieces of birch or other interesting bark*
- *6 grape tendrils, gilded*
- *several dried "hen of the woods" fungi*
- *24 to 36 ivy leaves, gilded*
- *1 spray can of high-gloss lacquer*

Instructions:

1. Refer to the instructions for "Making a Spanish Moss Base" on page 82 to complete the base for this wreath.

2. Cut pieces of sheet moss to fit the face of the moss base and glue them in place until the inside, face, and outside of the wreath base is covered.

3. Space the largest bark curls evenly on the wreath, wrapping them around the form if possible (see the photo of the finished product below). Glue them securely in place. On each side of the bark, glue a cluster of larch cones. Add the honeycomb in a conspicuous position.

4. Between the cones, place small pieces of reindeer moss, feathers, acorns, birch bark, grape tendrils, fungi, and finally the gilded ivy leaves, gluing them in place. Spray the wreath with a high-gloss lacquer to bring out the textures and subtle colors.

Woodland Bark and Moss Wreath, Fall Wall Basket.

11 Holiday and Winter Designs

MOONLIGHT WREATH

Moonlight Wreath.

MATERIALS

- *1 14-inch wire-form base*
- *4 to 5 bunches of German statice*
- *florist wire*
- *4 sensitive fern fronds*
- *1 can of metallic-gold spray paint*
- *2 1-foot lengths of ivy, dried*
- *hot glue gun*
- *1 premade bow in white, ivory, or metallic gold*
- *18 white helichrysum heads*
- *15 pearly everlasting heads*
- *1 small bunch of wild quinine*
- *1 small of bunch lunaria pods*
- *1 small bunch of white annual statice*
- *24 ammobium heads and 18 white gomphrena heads*

Instructions:

1. Refer to the instructions "Making a Wire-Form Base" on page 80 to make the wire base for this wreath.

2. Trim the German statice to lengths averaging 4 inches and make a pile to work from. Refer to the instructions "Making a Handwired Wreath" on page 85 to complete the German statice base for this wreath.

3. Spray the fern fronds with the metallic-gold spray paint. Spray the ivy in this way: Hold the ivy away from the paint can and spray using short bursts of paint. The result should be that the paint leaves the ivy with a dusting or spattering of gold.

4. Cut the fern frond stems to about four inches. Using hot glue, place them on the wreath at the extreme bottom, two fronds on one side and two fronds on the other (refer to the photo of the finished piece on page 133). Glue one end of each of the lengths of ivy to the wreath base just above the fern fronds. Position the ivy so that it encircles the side of the wreath, working along toward the top (again refer to photo). Glue into place where necessary.

5. Glue the bow to the wreath base just above the fern fronds.

6. Place and glue the helichrysum flowers on the wreath base, spacing them evenly and keeping them to the center of the statice. Place and glue the pearly everlastings, working them in between the helichrysum flowers. Trim the wild quinine and place the flowers to the inside and the outside of the wreath base throughout.

7. Trim off individual lunaria pods and glue them in place around the perimeter of the wreath.

8. Using the annual statice, gomphrena, and ammobium, fill between the larger flowers.
Note: When the German statice on this wreath fades too much to be attractive, try dusting it with gold metallic spray paint to extend the life of the wreath.

PRINCESS PINE CHRISTMAS WREATH

This beautiful Christmas wreath is made of recycled holiday roping and will last for many seasons.

MATERIALS

- *3 to 5 feet of last year's princess pine roping*
- *green fabric dye and a dye pot*
- *1 crimp-ring wreath, 10 inches or more*
- *holiday ribbon bow*
- *hot glue gun*
- *3 3-inch cinnamon sticks*
- *5 gold jingle bells*
- *1 small bunch of baby's breath, white or natural*
- *1 bunch of yarrow, dyed red*
- *6 bunches of pepperberries*
- *18 small pine cones, natural or gilded*
- *1 bunch of foxtail millet or other wild grass*

Instructions:

1. Refer to the instructions on page 74 for "Dying Flowers and Foliage" and dye the princess pine roping deep green. When it is nearly dry, yet still pliable, refer to "Using Crimp-Ring Wreath Forms" on page 87 and complete the base for this wreath.
2. Select a spot for the bow and glue it securely in place. Glue in the cinnamon sticks right next to the bow, leaving the ends showing as in the wreath pictured. Glue the jingle bells on, placing them next to the bow.
3. Make a small bundle of baby's breath, then wrap glue around the stem ends. Tuck the bundle under the princess pine foliage next to the bow, leaving only the flowers showing. Continue placing these bundles throughout the wreath—work them into the foliage all over the wreath surface, spacing them evenly throughout. Keep the bundles uniform in size and trim—do not make them overly large. Start near the bow and work in one direction until the wreath is studded with baby's breath.
4. Break the dyed yarrow heads into usable sizes and glue them on the wreath, working them throughout the entire wreath surface. Place and glue

Princess Pine Christmas Wreath.

in the pepperberries, keeping them to the outside of the wreath. Glue small clusters of pine cones to the inside and outside of the wreath.

5. Cut the stems of the foxtail millet to three inches and glue throughout the wreath, leaving the seed heads exposed.

CINNAMON STICK BUNDLE

These charming, old-fashioned decorations add the perfect touch to a mantel, coffee table, or end table during the holidays.

MATERIALS

- *small scraps of heavy-duty cardboard and enough felt to cover the bottom*
- *hot glue gun*
- *1 package of 12-inch cinnamon sticks*
- *Spanish moss*
- *1 premade bow in the color of your choice*
- *1 small bunch of statice latifolia*
- *small assortment of dried flowers; helichrysum, gomphrena, ammobium, annual statice, pearly everlastings, immortelle, hare's tail grass, or flowers of your choice in shades of the same color*
- *1 small stem of boxwood or other foliage, dyed forest green*

Instructions:

1. Cut a small piece of cardboard one inch by three inches for a six-inch bundle. Cover the back of the cardboard with felt, using hot glue. This will be the bottom of the piece; the felt will protect your table top.
2. Break the cinnamon sticks into uneven lengths from three to six inches. Begin by gluing sticks across the width of the cardboard base. Build up the cinnamon sticks to a height of about three inches by gluing on additional sticks. It will take quite a bit of glue to hold them in place. Glue on one layer and wait until the glue has cooled before gluing on the following layer. Make sure that the layer you have just glued in place is secure before you proceed with the next one.
3. When the cinnamon stick base is complete, glue a narrow rope of Spanish moss across the center width of the bundle. This is where you will place the flowers. Glue the bow on securely at the back of the bundle.
4. Place and glue on the largest flowers you will be working with. Fill in until the moss is covered with the smaller flowers. Trim off any excess Spanish moss.
5. Use small stems of dyed boxwood or other foliage as an accent throughout. Glue in small stems of statice latifolia to give the bundles a wispy appearance.

FROSTED HANGING PINE CONES

This unusual pine cone decoration uses a special wax to create the icicles.

MATERIALS

- *5 pounds of Lammo Wax*
- *coffee can*
- *newspapers*
- *1 large, perfect pine cone, exactly what kind does not matter as long as the base is flat*
- *1 premade large bow, 2 4-inch streamers, and a hanging loop in the holiday ribbon of your choice*
- *drill*
- *1 large screw eye*
- *small amount of Spanish moss*
- *hot glue gun*
- *forest green (dyed) boxwood, running cedar, or other foliage*
- *small assortment of dried flowers in the color of your choice*

TIP: Lammo Wax is a special wax designed to build layers of wax quickly. It should be available from candle-making supply houses or small candle-makers. If you cannot find Lammo Wax, try regular paraffin—it will just take longer to build up enough layers to achieve this look.

Instructions:

1. Melt the Lammo Wax in a coffee can that your pine cone will fit into. Place the can in a pan of hot water on a stove top.
2. Spread newspapers under your work area to catch any dripping wax. While you wait for the wax to melt, prepare the cone. Drill a hole in the bottom end for the screw eye. Screw it in securely.
3. Dip the cone into the melted wax and let the wax that builds up cool. Dip again and repeat until you have achieved the desired look. Allow the wax to harden completely.
4. Tie a length of ribbon through the screw eye to make a hanging loop. Make a bed of Spanish moss and glue it securely on the top of the cone. Glue the ribbon streamers in place, one on each side of the cone. Glue the bow to the moss, at the back edge of the cone.

Frosted Hanging Cone, Cinnamon Stick Bundle.

5. Next glue on a bed of foliage over the Spanish moss, then arrange and glue on the larger flowers you have chosen to use. Fill in with smaller flowers, adding more foliage to fill in if necessary.

HOLIDAY BOXWOOD WREATH AND GARLAND

Wreath

MATERIALS

- *1 10-inch wire-form base*
- *4 to 6 bunches of fresh boxwood*
- *florist wire*
- *green fabric dye and dye pot*
- *1 bunch of fresh German statice*
- *hot glue gun*
- *15 white helichrysum flowers*
- *12 pearly everlasting flowers, dyed country blue*
- *24 gomphrena flowers, dyed country blue*

Instructions:

1. Refer to the instructions "Making a Wire-Form Base" on page 80 for this wreath. Cut the boxwood stems to lengths averaging four inches until you have a nice pile to work from. Refer to the instructions "Making a Handwired Wreath" on page 85 to complete the boxwood base for this wreath. Be sure to pull the wire tightly around the boxwood—the stems are quite a bit more substantial than most fillers.

2. Refer to the instructions for "Dying Flowers and Foliage" on page 74 to dye the wreath base. You will be immersing the entire base at once into the dye pot. Allow the base to dry almost completely before continuing with the wreath.

3. Cut the stems of the German statice to lengths of about three inches. Glue the statice into place in the center of the wreath. Start in one place and work around in one direction. Leave only the flowers showing and be sure to face the flowers out to the viewer.

4. Glue white helichrysum flowers in the gaps between the sprays of German statice. Glue dyed pearly everlastings, then gomphrena flowers, to the inside and outside edges of the boxwood base.

Boxwood Wreath and Garland.

Garland

MATERIALS

- *40-inch length of sturdy twine*
- *florist wire*
- *2 to 3 bunches of fresh boxwood*
- *hot glue gun*
- *remainder of the German statice from the wreath above*
- *green fabric dye and dye pot*
- *12 heads of pearly everlasting, dyed country blue*
- *8 white helichrysum heads*
- *24 gomphrena flowers, dyed country blue*

Instructions:

1. Refer to the instructions "Making a Garland" on page 97 to make the boxwood base for this garland. You will have to keep extra tension on the twine as you work, because the boxwood is stiff.
2. Refer to the instructions for "Dying Flowers and Foliage" on page 74 to dye the garland base. After removing the garland from the dye pot, lay it flat on several sheets of newspaper and allow it to dry almost completely before you continue with this garland.
3. Cut the statice stems to three-inch lengths and glue into the garland, placing the stems along the bottom of the garland. Break the pearly everlasting into small bunches. Glue several small bunches to the garland just above the statice, leaving space between the flowers. Glue the white helichrysum to the garland. Fill in between the two main flowers with the gomphrena flowers.

VICTORIAN FLOWER CHRISTMAS WREATH AND TREE

This elegant twosome will dress up any room during the holidays.

Wreath

MATERIALS

- *1 12-inch artificial wreath base*
- *1 can of forest-green spray paint*
- *2 premade mauve bows in the ribbon style of your choice*

- *12 heads of hydrangea, natural*
- *hot glue gun*
- *24 helichrysum flowers in shades of white and pink*
- *1 bunch of statice latifolia*

Instructions:

1. Prepare the wreath base as described in "Embellishing Artificial Bases" on page 100. Place and glue the bows onto the wreath base.

2. Mist the hydrangea and let soften. Break the flowers down into large pieces. Make large bundles of hydrangea, being sure to pinch and roll the stems between your fingers to get nice full bunches. Glue each bunch in place in the center of the wreath surface, leaving a couple of inches between each bunch.

3. Place and glue the helichrysum flowers throughout the wreath base, spacing them well.

4. Cut the statice latifolia down to lengths about four inches long and glue into place, just catching the glue in the artificial foliage. Put enough *Statice latifolia* on the wreath base to give it a Victorian, frilly look.

Tree

This tree is worked in four layers. The key to making it successfully lies in being able to space your materials evenly throughout the tree, and knowing when to stop adding materials.

MATERIALS

- *1 18-inch artificial tree with sturdy base*
- *50 ribbon loops, cut from the ribbon of your choice*
- *25 helichrysum flowers in shades of mauve and white*
- *hot glue gun*
- *25 gomphrena flower heads in shades of pink*
- *12 hydrangea heads, natural*
- *1 bunch of statice latifolia*

Instructions:

1. Prepare the tree as described in "Embellishing Artificial Bases" on page 100.

2. Before cutting the ribbon loops for the tree, know two things: Loops should be narrow as compared with the ribbon bows on the matching pieces, or they will look odd; and a stiff flora-satin is best so that the ribbon loops will not droop. Next cut a narrow piece of cardboard eight inches long. Wrap the ribbon around the cardboard twenty-five times and cut.

Victorian Flower Christmas Wreath and Tree.

Now cut through the looped ribbon on each end of the cardboard—this will leave you with fifty times eight-inch pieces of ribbon. Make a double loop out of each piece and staple the end of the ribbon to hold the loops.

3. Begin placing the ribbon loops on the bottom tier of the tree. The entire tree is worked in four layers, so each component is put on in four layers, roughly speaking. Dab a ribbon loop with a bit of hot glue, then place it under a branch on the lower row of branches. As you place the loop, pinch the branch downward. Skip a few branches and place another loop. When you finish this bottom row, skip a row of branches and begin placing loops again. Try to place the loops as evenly as possible, adding more if necessary.

4. When all the ribbon loops are placed, start over on the bottom of the tree placing the helichrysum flowers. Glue them on the end of a branch that has a ribbon loop on it, skipping every other loop. Space them evenly throughout the tree. When you run out of helichrysum, go back and fill the skipped loops with the gomphrena flowers.

5. Spray the hydrangea flowers with water and allow them to soften. Break apart the flowers to make medium-sized bunches. Be sure to pinch and roll the stems between your fingers to make nice, full bunches. You will be placing the hydrangea on in four tiers. Begin by placing the first tier at the bottom of the tree. Dab glue on the hydrangea stems and push them into the foliage just above the lowest branches. The flowers should be behind the helichrysum flowers, but should not be pushed to the center of the tree (see photo of the finished piece on page 143). Make a full tier of solid hydrangea, then move to the next level. Continue until all four layers are in place.
6. Break the statice into stems about eight inches long and place them in the tree to give it a Victorian look. The statice flowers should not stand out from the tree foliage too far. Place it on the tree in four layers as you did the hydrangea.

PINE CONE WREATHS

This method for making pine cone wreaths allows you to use a variety of cones and other items. It also allows you to make a wreath of any size or shape you like—as long as the wreath base can hold the weight of the cones. I have made wreaths as tiny as three inches and as large as three feet across. If you attempt a wreath that large, be sure to have someone cut you a wooden base.

MATERIALS

- *1 15-inch heavy-duty cardboard wreath base, wrapped with fabric*
- *an assortment of pine cones in large, medium, and small sizes*
- *an assortment of woody natural items: sweet gum balls, acorns, peach pits, cotton pods, chestnuts, and the like*
- *1 spray can of high-gloss lacquer*

Instructions:

1. Refer to the instructions for "Making a Cardboard Base" on page 84 to complete the base for this wreath. This base should be wrapped in fabric.
2. Place the large and medium-sized assorted cones on your work table. Choose three or four large cones and several medium-sized cones from the pile to start with.
TIP: As you work, some cones should be placed on their sides, others upside down, and so on to show them to their best advantage. Some cones

should be placed to overlap the inner or outer edge of the wreath base—it should not be perfectly even around the edges. To make up the difference in height between large and small cones, small and medium cones should be built up in layers.

3. Begin with the largest cone you have chosen. Choose a spot for it on the wreath and glue it in place. Next, place the other large cones, spacing them evenly through the wreath. Fill in with the medium-sized cones, then choose more from the assortment. Continue to fill until none of the wreath base shows.

4. Check the inner and outer edge of the wreath to be sure that these edges do not show. If they do, go back and place small cones around the edges until they are no longer visible.

5. Check the wreath looking straight down on it. There should be no gaps showing between cones, and there should be no huge differences between the heights of the cones. Go back and fill in where necessary, this time using a few of the acorns, sweet gum balls, and other woody items you have accumulated. Fill with these items until you are content that all gaps have been covered and the wreath is full.

Pine Cone Wreaths.

6. To bring out the wood tones of this wreath, spray it with a high-gloss lacquer spray—commonly available at hardware stores. The wreath can be touched up with a fresh coat of lacquer each year.

FLORAL OR PINE CONE KISSING BALL

Floral and Pine Cone Kissing Balls.

This is such a wonderfully old-fashioned piece, perfectly suited for the holidays. The technique is the same for a kissing ball whether you choose to make it out of flowers or pine cones.

MATERIALS FOR FLOWER KISSING BALL

- *hot glue gun*
- *Spanish moss*
- *1 4-inch Styrofoam ball*
- *an assortment of flowers in shades of the same color*
- *1 2-inch "T" pin*
- *satin ribbon bow, streamers, hanging loop in the color of your choice*
- *an assortment of flowers in ivory and white*
- *statice latifolia*

MATERIALS FOR PINE CONE KISSING BALL

- *hot glue gun*
- *Spanish moss*
- *1 4-inch Styrofoam ball*
- *satin ribbon bow, streamers, hanging loop in the color of your choice*
- *1 can of spray paint in the color of your choice (optional)*
- *1 2-inch "T" pin*
- *an assortment of small pine cones; they need not all be the same, but the height of the cones should be fairly constant to keep the silhouette from being lumpy*

Instructions:

1. Glue a thin layer of Spanish moss to the Styrofoam ball. This will give the flowers/cones something to adhere to. Cut the ribbon streamers and glue them in place on the top of the ball where the hanging loop is to go. Cut the hanging loop, and using the "T" pin, pin it to the ball. Glue the bow in place in front of the hanging loop.

2. From your flower or cone assortment, choose the largest flowers/cones that you will be using. Glue them to the ball, spacing them evenly around the ball.

3. Now, fill in between the larger flowers or cones with the medium- and small-sized flowers or cones from your assortment. Fill one area at a time, then move on to the next. If you are using flowers, be sure to work ivory or neutral flowers in between the colored flowers. This will make the colors and the individual flowers themselves stand out a great deal more than they otherwise would. Continue in this fashion until all the gaps are filled.

4. Cut short stems of statice latifolia to use as accents for the flower kissing ball. Glue them in between the flowers, making sure that you place the flowers in a way so that they flow with the outline of the ball.

5. If you have made a pine cone kissing ball, you may spray it with a high-gloss lacquer or you may dust it with a chosen color. To dust it, pull up the streamers and bow so that the paint does not hit them. Hold the ball away from you and the spray paint about two feet from the kissing ball. Spray in short bursts of paint—this should just spatter the ball with color.

Spring and Summer Designs

VICTORIAN BIRD CAGE

MATERIALS

- *3 9-inch wire-form wreath bases*
- *floral tape*
- *florist wire*
- *Spanish moss*
- *1 bunch of faded German statice, dyed mauve*
- *hot glue gun*
- *1 feather bird*
- *10 to 12 yards of ivory or pink satin ribbon*
- *several stems of boxwood, dyed forest green*
- *24 white or pink helichrysum flowers*
- *24 pink or rose gomphrena flowers*

Instructions:

1. Refer to the instructions for "Making a Wire-Form Base" on page 80 to complete the two forms needed for this piece.

2. Place one base inside the other, and space them evenly apart. Wrap the spots where they overlap both top and bottom with floral tape to hold. Use a short piece of wire to reenforce and strengthen this juncture on the top and bottom of the forms.

Summer Flower Basket, Victorian Bird Cage.

3. Attach the florist wire to the forms at the top. Refer to the instructions "Making a Spanish Moss Base" on page 82 and proceed to wrap the entire form with moss, making each loop about one inch thick with moss.

4. Glue the end of the ribbon to the bottom of this form. Wrap each spoke with satin ribbon wound around like a candy stripe. Make a hanging loop, bow, and streamers of the remaining ribbon. Glue the streamers, then the bow, to the top of the form. Loop the hanging loop under a wire and tie into a loop.

5. The form should sit flat on your work surface. Cut the statice down into stems about two inches long. Using the photo as a guide, glue these small stems of statice around each spoke of the form. Tuck the end with glue on it just under the moss so that the glue will not show in the finished piece. Cut the boxwood into similar size pieces and glue them around each loop, next to the statice.

6. Glue the helichrysum flowers up the outside of each spoke of the form. Fill in between the helichrysum flowers with gomphrena.

7. Glue the feather bird into the center of the form.

SUMMER FLOWER BASKET

MATERIALS

- *1 small white basket*
- *Sahara foam to fit*
- *1 small bunch of Sweet Annie*
- *premade bow (optional)*
- *1 or more bunches of the following dried flowers: immortelle, natural or dyed santolina, natural or dyed yarrow, salvia, chives, achillea the pearl, lavender, bee balm, hare's tail grass, or any other flowers on the stem that appeal to you*

Instructions:

1. Refer to the instructions "How to Fill a Basket" on page 101. Outline the shape of the basket using the Sweet Annie by just placing it in the foam. Place the largest flowers next. Set the outer parameters of the arrangement with yarrow and any other larger flowers you may be using.

2. Using successively smaller flowers, begin to fill in the gaps. Spread the flowers around, placing one here and one there throughout the arrangement, then move on the next smallest flower and repeat the process. Continue until the foam is no longer visible. If you have difficulty reaching this point, you are probably placing your flowers too close together. Try adding more Sweet Annie and continue.

3. A bow may be tied to the handle of the arrangement or may be glued to the front of the basket.

ROSEBUD TOPIARY, WREATH, AND POMANDER

Topiary

MATERIALS

- *1 2-inch Styrofoam ball*
- *1 length of cured topiary wood*
- *1 4-inch clay pot*
- *Spanish moss*
- *hot glue gun*
- *several dozen miniature rosebuds*
- *patching plaster*
- *sheet moss*

Instructions:

1. Refer to the instructions for "Topiary Construction" on page 99 and prepare the topiary head. Cover the head with a thin layer of Spanish moss.
2. Turn the topiary upside down and begin on the bottom. Glue the rosebuds to the topiary head in concentric circles away from the trunk. When you have completed a bit, right the topiary and continue. Try to glue the rosebuds on in a regular, controlled manner—they should almost look as though they are lined up in rows.
3. Continue gluing until the topiary head is finished. Set the topiary in patching plaster as discussed on page 100. Finish the base by placing sheet moss over the top of the plaster. You may place a satin ribbon bow at the foot of the topiary if you wish.

Wreath

Rosebud Topiary, Wreath, and Pomander.

MATERIALS

- *1 6-inch Spanish moss wreath base*
- *1 satin ribbon bow in nearly the same color as the rosebuds*
- *hot glue gun*
- *several dozen rosebuds*
- *several stems of statice latifolia*

Instructions:

1. Refer to the instructions for "Making a Spanish Moss Base" on page 82 to complete a heart-shaped base for this wreath.
2. Place the bow on the top of the heart-shaped base and glue in place. Spread the bow.
3. Leave a short stem on the rosebuds. Begin gluing them to the wreath base in this order: Make a ring of buds around the outside edge, then the inside edge. Fill in an orderly fashion until the entire wreath base is filled with rosebuds.
4. Cut several short stems of statice latifolia and glue them on the base just under the bow. Fan out the pieces as shown in the photo of this wreath (page 151).

Pomander

MATERIALS

- *1 ribbon loop in nearly the same color as the rosebuds, straight pin*
- *1 2-inch Styrofoam ball*
- *Spanish moss*
- *hot glue gun*
- *several dozen rosebuds*

Instructions:

1. Make a loop of the ribbon and place the straight pin through the two cut ends. Push the pin into the Styrofoam ball, forming the hanging loop.
2. Cover the Styrofoam ball with a thin layer of Spanish moss. Glue the rosebuds onto the ball, referring to the instructions under this heading for making the Rosebud Topiary.

LIVING HERB AND FLOWER TABLE WREATH

Although not a dried flower piece, this wreath is easily made if you have flower gardens. It is the perfect centerpiece for an informal wedding, party, or any occasion. Because it is made of fresh in-season flowers, it is unique each time you make it.

MATERIALS

- *1 foam-filled 12-inch wreath form for a fresh wreath (may be purchased from a floral supply or craft store)*
- *1/2 bushel of fresh herb foliage and perennial foliage in season*
- *fresh flowers in season*

Instructions:

1. Soak the wreath form in cool water several hours or overnight. The wreath form is packed with floral foam and this takes a long time to soak up enough water to sustain flowers and foliage. Allow the base to drain for one hour before you start work.

Living Wreath, Summer Elegance Baby's Breath Wreath.

2. Bring the foliage to the work table; it should be absolutely fresh. You will be working with several types of foliage to create the base for a few flowers. Sort the foliage into piles of like foliage. Refer to the instructions for "Making a Wreath on a Straw Form" on page 89 for the correct working order for this piece.

3. Begin on the inside with one type of foliage. Cut a new, pointed end and keep the stems less than four inches in length. When you have inserted four to six stems, move to another type of foliage and use it. Keep working back and forth with the different foliages to mix them up. To use them to their best advantage, place contrasting foliages next to each other.

4. When the inside has been finished, repeat these steps for the face and then the outside of the wreath. Check to see that all the foam is covered. Pick more foliage as needed.

5. When all three sides of the wreath are filled, pick and add the flowers. A few larger flowers surrounded by smaller flowers that are light and airy always look better than placing flowers over the entire surface.

Note: You may keep these wreaths fresh for a week or so by placing them in the refrigerator when they are not in use. Flowers may be replaced as they fade.

SUMMER ELEGANCE BABY'S BREATH WREATH

MATERIALS

- *1 12-inch straw wreath form*
- *greening pins*
- *10 to 12 bunches of baby's breath, natural*
- *1 can of ivory spray paint*
- *1 bunch of natural or dyed German statice*
- *hot glue gun*
- *several stems of larkspur or astilbe (sprayed)*
- *several stems of Sweet Annie*
- *several stems each of annual statice in pink, white, and rose*
- *2 bunches of nigella pods*
- *2 bunches of sage or other herb foliage*
- *1 bunch of achillea the pearl*
- *24 helichrysum flowers in shades of pink or ivory*
- *24 gomphrena flowers in white, pink, and rose*
- *36 heads of field yarrow, natural*
- *several stems of dyed boxwood*
- *1 small bunch of statice latifolia*

Instructions:

1. Refer to the instructions for "Making a Wreath on a Straw Form" on page 89 to complete the baby's breath base for this wreath. Spray the base with the ivory spray paint.
2. Cut the stems of the German statice to lengths of about six inches. Place them in the wreath base a couple of inches apart and near the outer edge of the wreath. When you are satisfied with the arrangement, glue them into place.
3. At each spot where there is a piece of German statice, place and glue in a stem of larkspur cut to size. The larkspur should radiate out toward the edge of the wreath. Glue in a stem of Sweet Annie next to each larkspur stem.
4. Just to the inside of the flowers you have placed, place and glue securely an annual statice head (the entire flower). Vary the colors as you work around the wreath. Next to the statice flowers, glue two nigella pods.
5. In the center (from side to side) of the baby's breath, place small bunches of sage at intervals throughout the wreath (there should be two sage tips in each bunch). Leave two inches or so between bunches.
6. Place and glue small bunches of achillea between the bunches of sage randomly. Place the helichrysum flowers, working them in between the sage and achillea. When you are satisfied with their arrangement, glue them into place.
7. Work the gomphrena and field yarrow into the wreath between the larger flowers. Cut short stems of boxwood and place them throughout the wreath. Cut short stems of statice latifolia and place them randomly over the surface of the wreath.

SOUTHWESTERN WREATH

MATERIALS

- *artificial wreath base, 14 inches or larger*
- *1 can of forest-green spray paint*
- *florist wire*
- *2 or 3 bunches of statice latifolia, half sprayed sage green, half sprayed ivory*
- *several pieces of bleached driftwood or cholla from the desert*
- *hot glue gun*
- *2 or 3 bunches of yarrow, dyed or sprayed brick red and royal blue*

- *2 or 3 bunches of teasels, sprayed or dyed brick red and royal blue*
- *4 to 8 resin magnets depicting a southwestern theme such as a covered wagon, bleached skull, cactus, and the like*

Instructions:

1. Refer to the instructions for "Embellishing Artificial Bases" on page 100. Prepare the base; as described, enhance the base using the sprayed statice latifolia as a filler. Alternate sage green and ivory statice to create a mottled effect.

2. Cut or break the driftwood or cholla into usable pieces—do not make them so small that they get lost in the wreath. Glue them to the artificial base securely, spacing them evenly throughout and angling them from the inside to the outside of the wreath.

3. Cut the yarrow and teasel stems to about three inches. Place them evenly throughout the wreath and glue them in place securely.

Southwestern Wreath.

A southwestern wreath in progress.

4. Carefully glue the resin scenes into the wreath base. If they are too heavy to glue, drill a tiny hole in an inconspicuous place and wire them into place. You may wish to fill smaller pieces of yarrow between the larger flowers.

Note: Silk cactus, metal spurs, and other items reminiscent of the southwest can be added to this wreath.

SUMMER HERB WREATH

The base for this wreath can be used several times—just take off last season's herbs and flowers and rebuild the face of the wreath using fresh materials.

MATERIALS

- *1 12-inch crimp-ring form*
- *several bunches of Silver King artemisia*
- *4 or 5 bunches of rosebuds, dried on the stem*
- *4-inch floral picks*
- *fresh herb foliage in season: sage, lavender, Artemisia Stellerana (may substitute dusty miller), Russian sage, Sweet Annie, golden oregano, and/or lamb's ears*

- *fresh or dried herb flowers: monarda, oregano, wild quinine, chive, lavender, salvia, and/or roses*
- *hot glue gun*
- *1 or 2 bunches of achillea the pearl*
- *several stems of agastache flowers*

Instructions:

1. Refer to the instructions for "Using Crimp-Ring Wreath Forms" on page 87. Make the base for this piece of Silver King artemisia foliage and allow it to dry thoroughly.

2. Trim the herb foliages to about four inches in length, removing any damaged or discolored leaves. If you are working with foliage that is limp or does not have stiff stems, you may wish to place the foliage on 4-inch floral picks—this will make it easier to place in the wreath.

3. Begin tucking the trimmed herb foliage into the existing base of the wreath. Begin in one spot and work around the wreath in one direction. Use two or three stems of one foliage, then use another foliage working your way from the inside edge to the outside edge. Mix the foliage textures and colors to contrast with each other as you work.

4. When you have completed one row, place the next row of foliage so that it just covers the stems of the first. Work in this fashion until the entire wreath surface has been filled.

5. Place long-stemmed flowers like salvia, monarda, and lavender, arranging them along the outer edge of the wreath. In the center, glue in the stems of rosebuds in a circular fashion. Place the achillea the pearl just to the inside and outside of the rosebuds. Fill any remaining gaps in the wreath with salvia, lavender, agastache, and wild quinine.

CASPIA WREATH

MATERIALS

- *1 10-inch crimp-ring form*
- *2 large bunches of statice latifolia*
- *1 small bunch of Sweet Annie*
- *15 tulip seed heads, dyed mauve*
- *hot glue gun*
- *24 pearly everlasting heads, dyed mauve*
- *15 nigella pods, natural*
- *2 bunches of achillea the pearl*
- *1 bunch of pale pink annual statice*

Instructions:

1. Refer to the instructions for "Using Crimp-Ring Wreath Forms" on page 87 to complete the statice latifolia base for this wreath.
2. Cut the stems of the Sweet Annie to about six inches and insert them into the wreath so that they radiate to the outer edge like spokes. Leave two or three inches between stems. You may glue the stem ends in if you wish.
3. In the center of the statice (from side to side) place the dyed tulip seed heads, spacing them evenly throughout the wreath. Work in the dyed pearly everlasting flowers, leaving space between them and the seed heads. When you are satisfied with their arrangement, glue them in place.
4. Place the nigella pods just outside the dyed pearly everlasting flowers, spacing them evenly throughout the wreath. Work small bunches of achillea between the seed heads and the pearly everlastings. Add just a small amount of the annual statice to fill.

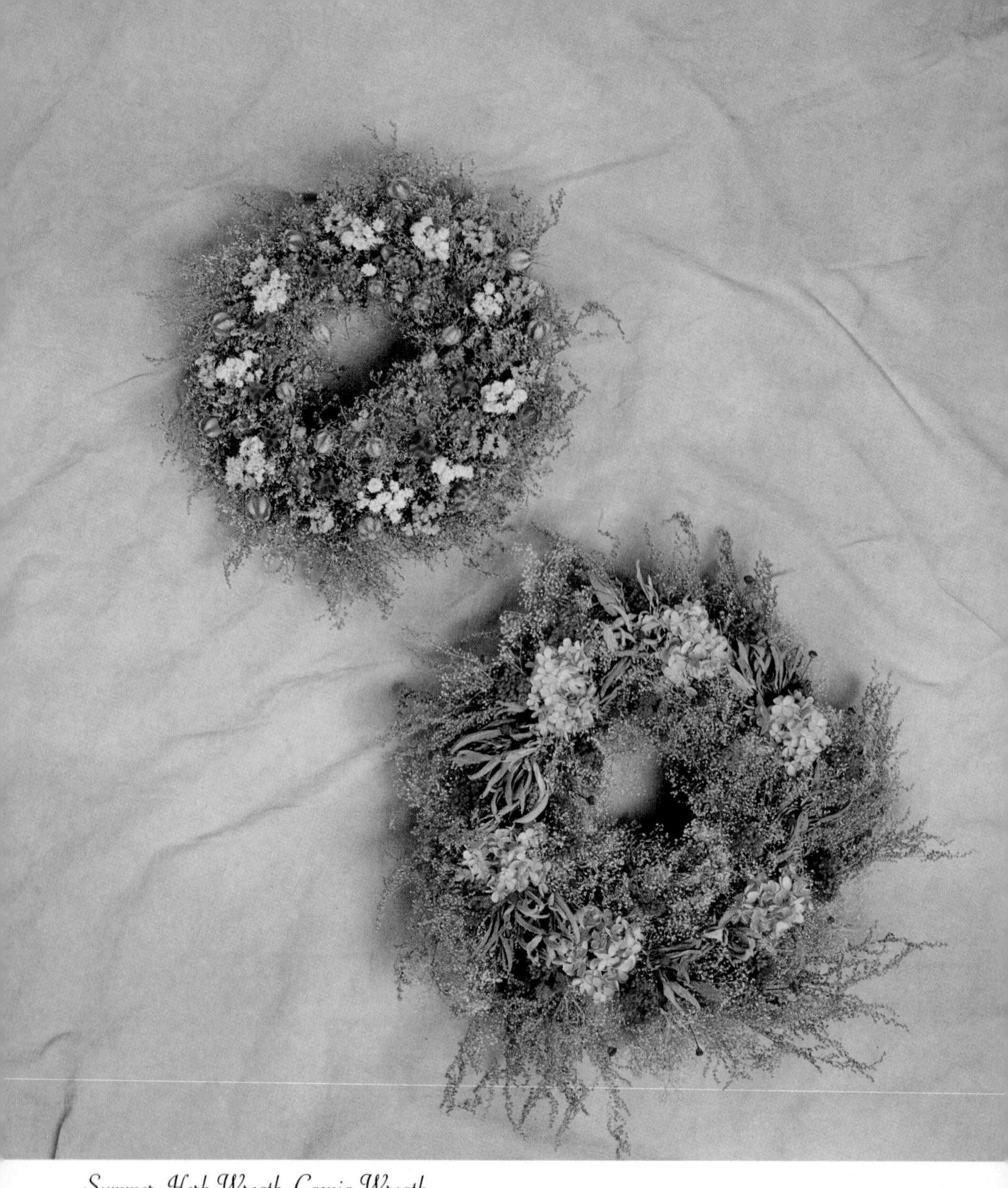

Summer Herb Wreath, Caspia Wreath.

Index